CW00665617

First Edition, October 1985.

ISBN 978-0-87083-187-4
(Messages 56-72, softcover)
ISBN 978-0-87083-188-1
(Complete set, softcover)

Published by

Living Stream Ministry
2431 W. La Palma Ave., Anaheim, CA 92801 U.S.A.
P. O. Box 2121, Anaheim, CA 92814 U.S.A.

Printed in the United States of America
09 10 11 12 13 14 / 12 11 10 9 8 7 6

Life-Study
of
Acts

Messages 56-72

Witness Lee

Living Stream Ministry
Anaheim, CA • www.lsm.org

CONTENTS

LIFE-STUDY OF ACTS

MESSAGE FIFTY-SIX

THE PROPAGATION
IN ASIA MINOR AND EUROPE
THROUGH THE MINISTRY OF PAUL'S COMPANY

(22)

Scripture Reading: Acts 21:1-26

After Paul's solemn and precious fellowship with the elders of the church in Ephesus (20:13-35), "he knelt down with them all and prayed" (20:36). Eventually, they escorted Paul to the ship. Acts 21:1 says, "Now it came about that when we parted from them and set sail, we took a straight course and came to Cos, and on the next day to Rhodes, and from there to Patara." The Greek word translated "parted" may also be rendered "tore ourselves."

At Patara Paul and his company found a ship crossing over to Phoenicia, went on board, and set sail (v. 2). They sailed to Syria and came down to Tyre. "And having sought out the disciples, we remained there seven days; and they told Paul through the Spirit not to set foot in Jerusalem" (v. 4). In 20:23 the Holy Spirit made known to Paul that bonds and afflictions awaited him in Jerusalem. The Holy Spirit's testifying concerning this was only a prophecy, a foretelling, not a charge. Therefore, Paul should have taken it not as a command but as a warning. Now in 21:4 the Spirit took a further step to tell him, through some members of the Body, not to go to Jerusalem. In practicing the Body life, Paul should have taken this word and obeyed it as a word from the Head.

TO PTOLEMAIS AND CAESAREA

Acts 21:7 and 8 go on to say, "And when we finished

the voyage from Tyre, we arrived at Ptolemais; and having greeted the brothers, we remained one day with them. And on the next day we went out and came to Caesarea; and entering into the house of Philip the evangelist, who was one of the seven, we remained with him." Wherever Paul went he visited the brothers and stayed with them (vv. 4-7). He was actually practicing the Body life of the church, living according to what he taught concerning the Body of Christ.

Acts 21:10 and 11 say, "And while we remained there many days, a certain prophet named Agabus came down from Judea. And he came to us and took Paul's girdle; and having bound his own feet and hands, he said, Thus says the Holy Spirit, In this way shall the Jews in Jerusalem bind the man whose girdle this is and deliver him into the hands of the Gentiles." Here the Holy Spirit told Paul again, not directly but through a member of the Body, what would befall him in Jerusalem. This was again a warning in the nature of a prophecy, not a charge. It was again the Head speaking through the Body, which Paul should have listened to in the practice of the Body life.

Verse 12 continues, "And when we heard these things, both we and those in that place entreated him not to go up to Jerusalem." The "we" includes Luke the writer. Here the Body, through many members, expressed its feeling, entreating Paul not to go to Jerusalem. But due to his strong will in being ready even to sacrifice his life for the Lord, he would not be persuaded. Concerning this, verse 13 says, "Then Paul answered, What are you doing, weeping and breaking my heart? For I am ready not only to be bound, but also to die in Jerusalem for the name of the Lord Jesus." Since Paul would not be persuaded, the members of the Body were forced to leave this matter to the will of the Lord. Verse 14 says, "And when he would not be persuaded, we were silent, having said, The will of the Lord be done."

TO JERUSALEM, ENDING THE THIRD JOURNEY

Acts 21:15 and 16 say, "And after these days, we got ready and went up to Jerusalem. And some of the disciples from Caesarea also went with us, bringing us to a certain Mnason of Cyprus, a disciple of long standing, with whom we were to lodge." In verse 16 we see that they were to lodge with Mnason in Jerusalem.

Verse 17 continues, "And when we had come to Jerusalem, the brothers welcomed us gladly." This coming to Jerusalem was the end of Paul's third ministry journey which began in 18:23.

THE INFLUENCE OF JUDAISM

A Mixture of God's New Testament Economy with the Old Testament Dispensation

According to 21:17, when Paul and his company came to Jerusalem, the brothers gladly welcomed them. Verse 18 says, "And on the following day Paul went in with us to James, and all the elders were present." The word "us" in this verse indicates that Luke was present.

In 21:18 we see that Paul went in to James. James was the central figure relating to the problem in Jerusalem, for he was a leader among the apostles and elders in Jerusalem. When Paul and his co-workers went in to see James, all the elders were present. This indicates that James was the leading one among the elders.

After Paul greeted the elders, "he related one by one the things which God did among the Gentiles through his ministry" (v. 19). Paul wisely did not teach them, but instead presented the things God had done through his ministry. When they heard this, they glorified God (v. 20).

Although the elders in Jerusalem glorified God for what He had done among the Gentiles through Paul's ministry, they nevertheless went on to say to him, "You observe, brother, how many thousands there are among the Jews who have believed, and all are zealous for the law." The Greek word rendered "thousands" also means myriads, ten thousands. These myriads of the Jews who believed were all zealous for the law.

The word in 21:20 about thousands of believing Jews being zealous for the law indicates how the Jewish believers in Jerusalem still kept the law of Moses, still remained in the Old Testament dispensation, and still were strongly under the Judaic influence, mixing God's New Testament economy with the out-of-date economy of the Old Testament.

James addressed his Epistle to "the twelve tribes in the dispersion" (James 1:1), indicating that it was written to Christian Jews. However, to call these believers in Christ "the twelve tribes," as God's chosen people in His Old Testament economy, may indicate the lack of a clear view concerning the distinction between Christians and Jews, between God's New Testament economy and the Old Testament dispensation. It may also indicate that James did not realize that God in the New Testament had delivered and separated the Jewish believers in Christ from the Jewish nation, which was then considered by God as a "crooked generation" (Acts 2:40). In His New Testament economy God no longer regards the Jewish believers as Jews for Judaism but as Christians for the church. Therefore, the Jewish believers, as the church of God, should be as distinct and separate from the Jews as from the Gentiles (1 Cor. 10:32). Nevertheless, James, as a pillar of the church (Gal. 2:9), in his Epistle to the Christian brothers, still called them "the twelve tribes." This was contrary to God's New Testament economy.

In his Epistle James also uses the word "synagogue" (James 2:2). The use of this word by James may indicate that the Jewish believers considered their assembly and assembling place as one of the synagogues among the Jews. James' use of this word in his Epistle may indicate that the Jewish Christians regarded themselves as still a part of the Jewish nation, as the chosen people of God according to the Old Testament, and that they lacked a clear vision concerning the distinction between God's chosen people of the Old Testament and the believers in Christ of the New Testament.

James 2:8-11 indicates that the Jewish believers at James' time were still practicing the keeping of the Old Testament law. These verses correspond to the word in Acts

21:20 spoken to Paul by James and the elders in Jerusalem concerning the zeal of the thousands among the Jews who believed for the law. James, the elders in Jerusalem, and many thousands of Jewish believers still remained in a mixture of the Christian faith and the Mosaic law. They even advised Paul to practice such a semi-Judaic mixture (21:20-26). They were not aware that the dispensation of law was altogether over and that the dispensation of grace should be fully honored, and that any disregard of the distinction between these two dispensations would be contrary to God's economical plan for the building up of the church as the expression of Christ.

In chapter twenty-one of Acts we see that James and the elders in Jerusalem had formed a mixture of God's New Testament economy with the Old Testament dispensation. Actually James and the elders were even promoting this mixture. Of course, they did not neglect faith in Christ, but they were still zealous for the Old Testament. As a result, there was a religious mixture in Jerusalem. We all need to have a clear understanding of this.

Paul Accused of Apostasy

Referring to the thousands of Jews who believed and were zealous for the law, James went on to say to Paul, "And they have been instructed concerning you that you are teaching all the Jews throughout the nations apostasy from Moses, telling them not to circumcise their children, nor to walk according to the customs" (v. 21). To leave the law of Moses, not to circumcise, and not to walk according to the customs of dead letters are really according to God's New Testament economy. But these were considered by the unbelieving Jews and even by the Jewish believers in Christ to be apostasy from God's Old Testament dispensation. It certainly is not apostasy to put aside the Old Testament economy. Rather, that is part of the carrying out of the truth. Nevertheless, James and the other elders used the situation among the thousands of believing Jews in Jerusalem in order to persuade Paul.

Those believing Jews who had been instructed concerning Paul were correct as to the facts, but they were mistaken in accusing Paul of apostasy. In the Epistle to the Galatians Paul clearly says that the law has been put aside, and that he is dead to the law: "I through law have died to law that I might live to God" (Gal. 2:19). This means that Paul no longer had anything to do with the law. For him to have died to the law means that the obligation under the law, the relationship to the law, was terminated. Hence, before Paul came to Jerusalem the last time in Acts 21, he had clearly written to the Galatians that he was dead to the law and had nothing to do with it.

The Jews were right regarding the facts, but they twisted the facts by accusing Paul of teaching apostasy. Apostasy is a matter of heresy. Paul's departure from the law was neither apostasy nor heresy; it was the practice of the truth of God's New Testament economy. However, the opposers took the facts and twisted them. Our opposers do the same thing today.

According to 21:21, Paul taught apostasy from Moses, telling the Jews not to circumcise their children nor to walk according to the customs. I believe that Paul did teach that it was no longer necessary to practice circumcision. Yet, as we have pointed out, he had Timothy circumcised (16:1-3). The criticism of his opposers, therefore, was not fair.

The Jews also claimed that Paul taught the people not to walk according to the customs. In this matter they were accurate. Nevertheless, the report that went to Jerusalem concerning Paul's ministry was only partially true. The situation is the same with us today.

The Requirement That Paul Be Purified
with Those Who Had a Vow on Themselves

In 21:22 and 23a James and the elders said to Paul, "What then is to be done? They will certainly hear that you have come. Therefore do what we tell you." Literally, the Greek word translated "what" means "this that." In verse 23 James and the elders did not propose something to Paul;

rather, they required it of him, telling him to do what they said to him.

James and the elders went on to say, "Four men are with us who have a vow on themselves; take these and be purified with them, and pay their expenses that they may shave their heads; and all will know that there is nothing to the things of which they have been instructed concerning you, but that you yourself also walk orderly, keeping the law" (vv. 23b-24). The vow mentioned in verse 23 was the Nazarite vow (Num. 6:2-5). For Paul to be purified with the Nazarites was to become a Nazarite with them, joining them in their vow. The word "purely" is used in the Septuagint in Numbers 6:3, in describing the Nazarite's duties. To take the Nazarite vow is a purification before God.

In addition to telling Paul to be purified with the four who had a vow on themselves, they told him to pay their expenses so that they might shave their heads. Paying their expenses refers to the cost of the offerings which a Nazarite had to pay for the completion of his purification (Num. 6:13-17). This was very expensive for the poor Nazarites. It was a custom among the Jews, and was considered a proof of great piety, that a rich person would pay the expenses of the offerings for the poor.

The shaving of the head was to be done at the completion of the Nazarite vow (Num. 6:18). This shaving differed from the shearing in Acts 18:18, which was for a private vow. We have emphasized the fact that the vow in 18:18 was a private vow in any place by the Jews for thanksgiving, with the shearing of hair. It differed from the Nazarite vow, which had to be carried out in Jerusalem with the shaving of the head. In Acts 18 Paul had a private vow, and it seems that God tolerated it, probably because it, being a private vow accomplished in a place other than Jerusalem, would not have had much effect on the believers.

Acts 21:26 says, "Then Paul took the men on the following day, and having been purified with them entered into the temple, giving notice of the completion of the days of the purification, until the offering was offered for each one of them." Here we see that Paul participated in their Nazarite vow. In order to do this, Paul had to enter into the temple and remain there with the Nazarites until the completion of the seven days of the vow. Then the priests would offer the offerings for each one of them, including him. Paul surely was clear that such a practice was of the out-of-date dispensation, which, according to the principle of his teaching in the New Testament ministry, should be repudiated in God's New Testament economy. Yet he went through with it, probably because of his Jewish background, which was also manifested in his earlier private vow in 18:18, and because he was practicing his word in 1 Corinthians 9:20. However, his toleration jeopardized God's New Testament economy, which God would not tolerate. As we shall see, just at the time when their vow was to be concluded, God allowed an uproar to rise up (v. 27).

God's Dealing with the Mixture in Jerusalem

The mixture of Judaic practices with God's New Testament economy was not only erroneous in God's dispensation, but also abominable in the eyes of God. This gross mixture was terminated by Him a mere ten years or so later with the destruction of Jerusalem and the temple, the center of Judaism, through Titus and his Roman army. This rescued the church and absolutely separated it from the devastation of Judaism.

God might have tolerated the private vow Paul had in 18:18, but He would not allow Paul, His chosen vessel not only for the completion of His New Testament revelation (Col. 1:25) but also for the carrying out of His New Testament economy (Eph. 3:2, 7-8), to participate in the Nazarite vow, a serious Judaic practice. Paul might have intended in going to Jerusalem to clear up the Judaic influence on the church there, but God knew that it was incurable. Hence, in His sovereignty He allowed Paul to be arrested by the Jews and imprisoned by the Romans so that he might write his last eight Epistles, which completed the divine revelation (Col. 1:25) and gave the church a clearer and deeper view concerning God's New Testament economy (Eph. 3:3-4). Thus, God left the Judaic-influenced church in Jerusalem to remain as it was until the devastating mixture was terminated with the destruction of Jerusalem. For Paul to write his last eight Epistles to complete God's New Testament revelation was far more important and necessary than for him to accomplish some outward works for the church.

LIFE-STUDY OF ACTS

MESSAGE FIFTY-SEVEN

THE PROPAGATION
IN ASIA MINOR AND EUROPE
THROUGH THE MINISTRY OF PAUL'S COMPANY

(23)

Scripture Reading: Acts 21:18-26

In this message we shall continue to consider Paul's situation in 21:18-26.

PURIFIED WITH THE NAZARITES

We have seen that, on the one hand, James and all the elders glorified God when they heard about the things God had done among the Gentiles through Paul's ministry (vv. 18-20a). On the other hand, they pointed out to Paul that in Jerusalem thousands of Jews believed and were zealous for the law (v. 20). Furthermore, these believing Jews had been instructed concerning Paul that he taught "apostasy from Moses, telling them not to circumcise their children, nor to walk according to the customs" (v. 21). James and the elders went on to make the following requirement of Paul: "Four men are with us who have a vow on themselves; take these and be purified with them, and pay their expenses that they may shave their heads; and all will know that there is nothing to the things of which they have been instructed concerning you, but that you yourself also walk orderly, keeping the law" (vv. 23-24). As we have seen, the vow mentioned here is the Nazarite vow (Num. 6:2-5). To be purified with the Nazarites was to become a Nazarite with them, joining them in their vow.

According to verse 24, Paul was told to be purified with the four men who had a vow on themselves and to pay their expenses. The first thing a Nazarite had to do was to purify himself in the presence of God. According to the custom at the time, the rich would often pay the expenses of the offerings needed for a Nazarite to complete his purification. Sometimes the poor Nazarites could not afford to pay for all the offerings. Thus, they needed someone to help them with the expenses. Those who helped the Nazarites in this way joined themselves to them.

Here in Acts 21, for Paul to be purified with the Nazarites and to pay their expenses was for him to be joined to them so that the four would then become five. In the words of James and the elders in Jerusalem, if Paul were to be purified with the Nazarites and pay their expenses, all the believing Jews would know that Paul himself also walked orderly, keeping the law. But was Paul keeping the law? He certainly was not keeping the law. Nevertheless, James and the elders told Paul to join himself to the four Nazarites so that the Jewish believers would see that he kept the law. This was a serious, terrible, and mistaken requirement made by James and the elders.

In 21:25 James and the elders said to Paul, "But concerning the Gentiles who have believed, we wrote, having decided that they should keep themselves from idol sacrifices and blood and anything strangled and fornication." Their word here has the same old tone as that in chapter fifteen.

Acts 21:26 says, "Then Paul took the men on the following day, and having been purified with them entered into the temple, giving notice of the completion of the days of the purification, until the offering was offered for each one of them." The completion spoken of here is the completion of the Nazarite vow (Num. 6:13).

I would call your attention to the word "having been purified." Here we see that Paul had already been purified with the four Nazarites. He then took them into the temple and waited with them for the offering to be offered for each one. This time of waiting is indicated by the word "until." Having been purified along with the four, Paul waited in the temple with them for the priest to come at the end of the completion on the seventh day to offer sacrifices for them all, including Paul.

PAUL'S COMPROMISE AND RELEASE

It is very difficult to believe that Paul would be purified, enter into the temple, and wait for the offerings to be offered by the priest. He did this after writing the Epistles to the Galatians and the Romans, books that were written not long before he came to Jerusalem. Although it is difficult to believe that Paul carried out the word of James and the elders, it is a fact that he joined himself to the Nazarites and went with them into the temple.

As we shall see in a later message, there was an uproar against Paul (21:27—23:15), and he was seized by the Jews in Jerusalem (21:27-30). Concerning this, 21:27 and 28 say, "Now when the seven days were about to be concluded, the Jews from Asia saw him in the temple and threw all the crowd into confusion; and they laid their hands on him, crying out, Men, Israelites, help! This is the man who is teaching all men everywhere against the people, and the law, and this place; and besides, he has even brought Greeks into the temple and has profaned this holy place." This uproar took place "when the seven days were about to be concluded," that is, on the seventh day. Humanly speaking, Paul's intention in going into the temple was to avoid trouble. Actually, his going into the temple with the four Nazarites caused a great deal of trouble for him.

Suppose Paul had decided not to go to the temple but simply to stay with the brothers in the house of Mnason, with whom Paul and his companions were to lodge in Jerusalem. Let us further suppose that Paul had said to the brothers, "I do not care for the temple, because God is finished with it. Brothers, did the Lord Jesus not tell us that God has forsaken the temple? I am practicing the Lord's word concerning us. The priesthood and all the sacrifices are also over. Therefore, I cannot go back to the temple to have any share in the offerings and the priesthood. Brothers,

I would like to stay here to have fellowship with you." Would not the situation have been very different if Paul had decided not to go to the temple and instead had spent his time having fellowship with the brothers? To be sure, the situation would have been very different.

In chapter twenty-one of Acts Paul was compromising. He was the writer of the Epistles to the Galatians and the Romans, yet not long after these Epistles were written, he took the step described in this chapter. For Paul to take such a step was a great compromise on his part.

According to 21:26 and 27, Paul was in the temple waiting for the completion of the days of the purification. He was to be in the temple until the priest came to offer the offerings for him and the four others. How could Paul bear to stay in the temple for that period of time? Do you think he was happy? Do you think he was joyfully praising the Lord? Paul could praise the Lord when he was in prison in Philippi (16:23-25). But do you think he could praise the Lord there in the temple in Jerusalem? Apparently, the temple was a much better place for Paul than a prison. However, that prison in Philippi actually became a holy place, even the heavens, for Paul, whereas the temple in Jerusalem was a prison for him. In a very real sense, Paul was imprisoned there in the temple, unable to be released. Paul had become "trapped" in that situation.

Although Paul was imprisoned in the temple, the Lord had a way to release him from this prison. The Lord used the Jews to accomplish this release. In particular, the Lord used the uproar caused by the Jews to take Paul out of the temple. On the one hand, Paul was then in greater difficulty. On the other hand, he was released not only from the temple but also from the God-condemned mixture of the New Testament grace with the Old Testament law in Jerusalem. In His sovereignty the Lord protected His faithful servant from that terrible mixture.

THE DESTRUCTION OF JERUSALEM

We have pointed out that Paul went to Jerusalem the last

time not only to carry out his loving concern for the need of the poor saints there, but also to have fellowship with James and the other apostles and elders in Jerusalem concerning the Judaic influence upon the church there. The decision made by the conference of the apostles and elders in Acts 15 to solve the problem concerning circumcision was not fully satisfactory to him. Therefore, in going to Jerusalem, Paul might have intended to clear up the Judaic influence on the church there. However, God had His own way to deal with the situation. In His sovereignty He allowed Paul to be arrested by the Jews and imprisoned by the Romans. He then allowed the terrible mixture of the grace with the law in Jerusalem to remain until the city was destroyed by Titus with his Roman army in A.D. 70. That mixture was terminated approximately ten years after the events recorded in Acts 21.

In the Gospel of Matthew the Lord Jesus prophesied the coming destruction of Jerusalem. For example, in the parable in Matthew 21:33-46 concerning the transfer of the kingdom of God, the Lord portrayed the leaders of the Israelites as evil husbandmen (vv. 33-35, 38-41), indicating that God would "miserably destroy those evil men, and will lease the vineyard to other husbandmen, who will render the fruits to him in their seasons." This word concerning destruction was fulfilled when Titus destroyed Jerusalem. The Lord also predicted the destruction of Jerusalem in the parable in Matthew 22:1-14. In Matthew 22:7 He says, "And the king was angry; and he sent his troops and destroyed those murderers and burned their city." These "troops" were the Roman soldiers under Titus who destroyed Jerusalem.

In Matthew 23:37-39 we see the Lord's forsaking of Jerusalem with its temple. Concerning the coming destruction of the temple, the Lord said to His disciples, "Do you not see all these things? Truly I say to you, A stone shall by no means be left upon a stone which shall not be thrown down" (Matt. 24:2). This also was fulfilled when Titus destroyed Jerusalem. According to the description given by Josephus, the destruction of Jerusalem and the temple was thorough and

absolute. Thousands of Jews were killed, perhaps including
many of the Jewish believers. In His anger the Lord not only
destroyed a rebellious nation of Israel; He also terminated
Judaism and the mixture of Judaism with Christianity.
When Jerusalem was destroyed, the source of the "poison"
that was flowing out of it was also terminated. Therefore,
the Lord had His marvelous way to deal with the situation
in Jerusalem.

THE LORD SOVEREIGNLY DELIVERING PAUL
AND TRANSFERRING HIM

The Lord knew what was in Paul's heart. He also knew
that Paul was faithful but was not able to help the situation.
Instead of helping it, Paul was trapped in it by compromising with it. However, the Lord used the uproar described
in 21:27—23:15 to rescue Paul. The Jews seized him and
were seeking to kill him (21:30-31). But a commander of the
Roman cohort intervened, laid hold of him, ordered him to be
bound with chains, and inquired concerning the situation
(21:31-33). It was not the commander's intention to protect
Paul. He was simply fulfilling his duty to maintain order in
the city. He could not allow such an uproar to continue.
Therefore, he intervened, and through his intervention Paul
was rescued. Actually, the commander's intervention was
Paul's protection from the plot of the Jews.

Through the intervention of the Roman commander, Paul
was given the opportunity to defend himself before the rioting Jews (21:40—22:21). Following that, he was bound by
the Romans (22:22-29) and defended himself before the
Sanhedrin (22:30—23:10). Because of the plot of the Jews
(23:12-15), Paul was transferred to the Roman governor in
Caesarea (23:16—24:27), where he remained in custody for
quite a period of time. Apart from God's sovereignty in using
the Roman commander to protect Paul, he would have been
killed. God sovereignly delivered Paul out of that threaten-
ing situation.

In His sovereignty the Lord caused Paul to have a
dispensational transfer. Paul was in favor of such a transfer.

He came to Jerusalem with the positive intention and strong purpose to help the believers there to experience this dispensational transfer. However, instead of helping them, he himself was eventually trapped in a situation of mixture and compromise. Paul must have been unhappy when he was in the temple with the four Nazarites, for he did not have a way out of the situation. Paul must have regretted joining those who had the Nazarite vow. He might have regretted going to the temple instead of staying in the house of Mnason with his co-workers, keeping himself away from the attention of the Jews. Paul, however, joined himself to the Nazarites and went with them into the temple, where he was seen by Jews from Asia and seized by them. Their intention was to kill him. Who except the Lord could help the situation? The Lord was sovereign and helped Paul to have a complete transfer out of the Judaic mixture in Jerusalem.

As a result of what happened in Jerusalem, Paul was taken to Caesarea and was probably kept there for two years. We may infer that those two years were a profitable and an excellent time for Paul. What do you think Paul did during those years in Caesarea? What did he do while he was being kept from both his work and from the trouble caused by the plotting Jews? He may have been preparing to write the crucial books of Ephesians, Philippians, Colossians, and Hebrews. While Paul was in custody in Caesarea, he might have considered putting into writing those materials that would complete his ministry. Thus far, Paul had written only six of his fourteen Epistles: Romans, Galatians, 1 and 2 Corinthians, and 1 and 2 Thessalonians. Although these books are basic, they are not as crucial as Ephesians, Philippians, Colossians and Hebrews. Before 1 and 2 Timothy, Titus, and Philemon were written, these four crucial books were written after Paul's two-year period of custody in Caesarea. Just as Paul's time in Arabia had much to do with the early part of his ministry, so the two years in Caesarea had a great deal to do with Paul's upcoming writings in the completion of his ministry.

We need to be impressed with the Lord's sovereignty in completing Paul's transfer from the old dispensation to the new. Praise the Lord that such a transaction took place! In His sovereignty and wisdom, the Lord carried out such a complete transfer with Paul, and this transfer is fully recorded in the holy Word. Having this record in our hands, we can now see a full pattern concerning the complete transfer from the Old Testament economy to God's New Testament economy.

LIFE-STUDY OF ACTS

MESSAGE FIFTY-EIGHT

THE PROPAGATION
IN ASIA MINOR AND EUROPE
THROUGH THE MINISTRY OF PAUL'S COMPANY

(24)

Scripture Reading: Acts 21:18-39

A SUMMARY OF THE REVELATION IN THE BIBLE

The Bible reveals that God had an eternal plan and that this plan eventually became His economy. God's plan is to have a group of human beings who are regenerated with the divine life become His sons and the members of Christ so that the Triune God in Christ may have a Body through which to express Himself.

God's plan is accomplished through Christ's incarnation, human living, and all-inclusive death to terminate everything of the old creation so that He may germinate His chosen people in resurrection. In His resurrection Christ became the life-giving Spirit (1 Cor. 15:45) so that He may propagate Himself as the processed Triune God to produce the Body. After His resurrection Christ ascended to the heavens, and there He was made the Lord and Christ (Acts 2:36). In His resurrection the Lord had already breathed Himself as the Spirit into His chosen people essentially (John 20:22). Then in His ascension He poured out Himself as the all-inclusive consummated Spirit upon them economically. Therefore, everything has been fulfilled and accomplished: incarnation, human living, the all-inclusive death, the life-giving and propagating resurrection, the breathing of the life-giving Spirit essentially, the ascension, and the pouring out of the consummated Spirit economically.

Because all this has been accomplished, the church has been produced.

Before Christ came to pass through the processes for accomplishing God's plan, the points related to it were put into the Old Testament in the way of promises, prophecies, types, figures, and shadows. Then, in the fullness of time, the Triune God in the Son became a man (Gal. 4:4). In His humanity He passed through the processes of human living, crucifixion, resurrection, and ascension to accomplish everything for the fulfillment of God's plan. Having become the all-inclusive Spirit, He now enters into God's chosen people to apply to them all that the Triune God in the Son has accomplished. Through such an application, God's people become living witnesses of the incarnated, crucified, resurrected, and ascended Christ (Acts 1:8).

As those who have the all-inclusive Spirit within us, what should we do? We should simply be living witnesses containing, bearing, and conveying the incarnated, crucified, resurrected, and ascended Christ so that He may be propagated throughout the earth for the fulfillment of the divine economy. This is a brief summary of the entire revelation in the New Testament.

THE SITUATION OF MIXTURE IN JERUSALEM

Since Christ has come and passed through the processes of incarnation, human living, crucifixion, resurrection, and ascension, breathing the Spirit into God's chosen people essentially and pouring the Spirit upon them economically, many of the promises, prophecies, types, figures, and shadows in the Old Testament related to this are now out-of-date. God's people should not hold on to these out-of-date things. However, degraded Judaism as a religion continues to hold on to those things which have become out-of-date.

Between those in degraded Judaism and the Christian believers was the situation of mixture in Jerusalem. In Jerusalem was the first group of vessels chosen by God to contain Christ. This group included the apostles, among whom Peter was the leading one and James was the most influential one. According to Acts 21, with these apostles there were thousands of Jews who believed in Christ (v. 20). Although they had become believers in Christ, they were still strongly under the influence of their Judaic background. Because of this influence, it was impossible for them to abandon their background and to give up the atmosphere that prevailed in Jerusalem.

The Jewish believers in Jerusalem became those who insisted on having both faith in Christ and also the out-of-date things of the Old Testament. They wanted to put these two matters together. I would say that, according to my study of the New Testament, James was the leader in this trend. It seems that he took the lead to say, "There is no need for us to fight. We may keep our faith in Christ and at the same time also keep the Old Testament laws, customs, and practices. We may still practice circumcision."

In not wanting to fight or offend others, James may have had a very good intention. He may have had a good heart in wanting to blend the Old Testament dispensation with faith in Christ. We also need to realize that James had a broadened heart. This is indicated by the fact that he did not propose that the Gentile believers be circumcised. Consider the solution he proposed to the problems concerning circumcision during the course of the fellowship recorded in Acts 15: "I judge that we do not harass those from the Gentiles who turn to God. But that we write to them to abstain from the pollutions of idols and fornication and what is strangled and blood. For Moses from ancient generations has in every city those who proclaim him in the synagogues, being read every Sabbath" (vv. 19-21). James made it clear that it was not necessary for the Gentiles to be circumcised or to keep the law. He only required that they abstain from idol worship, fornication, things strangled, and blood.

James, however, continued to think that it would be better for the Jewish believers to practice the things of the Old Testament and to keep the law. James seemed to say, "The Gentiles do not need to keep the law or to be circumcised. But we Jews should practice circumcision and keep the law. We need to practice the kind of life exactly like that practiced by our forefathers in the Old Testament. Of course, we now have faith in Christ. Therefore, let us keep both the Old Testament things and our faith in Christ." This, I believe, was James' concept.

A CLEAR VISION OF THE BODY

If James' concept had been widely accepted in Asia Minor and Europe, how could there have been one Body for Christ in a practical way? Would there be two kinds of churches—a Judaic church for the Jewish believers and a Gentile church for the Gentile believers? Such a thing is utterly impossible.

Concerning the Body Paul had seen a clear vision. He spoke of the one Body in Romans 12:5, and in 1 Corinthians 12:13 he said, "In one Spirit we were all baptized into one body, whether Jews or Greeks, whether slaves or free, and were all given to drink one Spirit." Furthermore, in Galatians 3:27 and 28 Paul said, "For as many as were baptized into Christ have put on Christ. There cannot be Jew nor Greek, there cannot be slave nor free man, there cannot be male and female; for you are all one in Christ Jesus." Although Paul had seen a clear vision, in his first six Epistles—Romans, Galatians, 1 and 2 Corinthians, and 1 and 2 Thessalonians—this vision was not yet presented in a full way. No doubt Paul was waiting for a time to put into writing the vision he had seen.

THE LORD'S SOVEREIGN RESCUE OF PAUL

When Paul saw the situation of mixture in Jerusalem, he must have been heavily burdened by it. Perhaps when James made his presentation to him in chapter twenty-one concerning the thousands of Jews who believed and who were zealous for the law and concerning Paul's joining with those who had the Nazarite vow, he was hesitating what to do. Perhaps he said to himself, "Humanly speaking, I should simply do what James says. After I pass through this critical time, I may have another opportunity to adjust or clarify the situation in Jerusalem." This may have been Paul's thought as he complied with James' proposal (21:23-26).

The Lord, however, did not allow Paul to complete the days of the purification. Paul, a chosen vessel, was the unique one used by the Lord to carry out God's New Testament economy. How could the Lord allow such a one to complete the days of purification, which involved the temple, the priesthood, and the offering of animal sacrifices with the shedding of blood? All these things were terminated by God's New Testament economy. The Lord could not tolerate this. Hence, almost at the last minute, at the time when Paul's vow was about to be completed, the Lord came in, and there was a great disturbance. That was the Lord's exercise of His sovereignty concerning Paul to rescue him from that dilemma.

In Acts 21 Paul was in danger of being killed, and he certainly must have been afraid of this. If the Roman commander had not intervened when he did, Paul certainly would have been put to death. But the Lord's sovereign hand controlled everything to rescue Paul from that situation and to preserve his life. Later, after Paul defended himself before the rioting Jews (21:40—22:21), was bound by the Romans (22:22-29), and defended himself before the Sanhedrin (22:30—23:10), he was encouraged by the Lord. According to 23:11, "the Lord stood by him and said, Take courage, for as you have solemnly testified concerning Me in Jerusalem, so you must also testify in Rome." This was a great encouragement to Paul and assured him that he would not be killed by the Jews. We all need to have a clear view of Paul's situation here at this point in Acts.

OUR NEED TO SEE GOD'S ECONOMY
AND TO HAVE A DISPENSATIONAL TRANSFER

At this point we need to go on to consider today's situation. As a whole, Christianity is not a testimony of the incarnated, crucified, resurrected, and ascended Christ. There is a great deal of mixture in Christianity, not just of the one element of Judaism, but also of many other elements. The mixture has gone to such an extent that among the millions of Christians very few know what God's New Testament economy is. For the most part, fundamental Christians know the redemption of Christ in a rather superficial way. In addition, they teach people to be ethical and moral in order to glorify God. Who among your Christian friends knows God's New Testament economy to propagate the resurrected Christ and to impart this Christ into the believers so that they may be living members to form Christ's Body in this age in order to express the Triune God? Where can you find believers who know this?

Because the majority of today's Christians have not seen the vision concerning God's New Testament economy in the Word, I am burdened in this Life-study of Acts to emphasize God's economy. It is not my burden to touch the many small points in this book. For example, someone has asked me why in Acts 18:18 and 26 Priscilla is mentioned before Aquila but in 1 Corinthians 16:19 Aquila is mentioned first and Priscilla last. I simply do not have the heart to cover these minor things. In my heart is the concern for the matter of a dispensational transfer. As we study the book of Acts, we should learn to say, "Lord, we need a great transfer, a dispensational transfer. We need to be transferred from degraded Judaism, Catholicism, and Protestantism into God's New Testament economy. We need a transfer from all religious things into the pure revelation of God's economy."

We need to see that God's intention is to propagate the resurrected Christ by imparting Him into us so that we may become His living members saturated with Him and constituted of Him in order that Christ may have a Body on earth for His expression. Then He will bring His kingdom in, and following that there will be the ultimate consummation of God's New Testament economy. Our need is to see this and to have a dispensational transfer so that we may be in it in a practical way.

In these messages it is not my burden merely to teach the Bible. Rather, I am burdened to present what the Lord, in His mercy, has shown us from the Word concerning the New

Testament economy of God. If we see this vision, we shall not care about opposition or attack. Those who oppose the Lord's recovery do not have the view, the vision, concerning God's New Testament economy. We cannot deny that we have seen this vision, and our testimony concerning it is becoming stronger and stronger. In our reading of Acts may we devote our full attention to and concentrate our entire being on the vision of God's New Testament economy.

LIFE-STUDY OF ACTS

MESSAGE FIFTY-NINE

THE PROPAGATION
IN ASIA MINOR AND EUROPE
THROUGH THE MINISTRY OF PAUL'S COMPANY

(25)

Scripture Reading: Acts 21:18-39; Matt. 17:1-8; Heb. 1:1-3; 2:14; 3:1; 8:6; 9:15; Eph. 1:17-23; 2:14-16; 3:8, 17-21; 4:4-6, 24; 5:18; 6:11; Phil. 3:4-14; Col. 1:12, 15, 18; 2:2, 9, 16-17; 3:4, 10-11; Rev. 2:7, 17; 3:5, 20

Before we go on in this Life-study to another section of the book of Acts, I would like to give a further word concerning the need for a dispensational transfer, the transfer out of the Old Testament economy into God's New Testament economy.

THE DISAPPEARING
OF THE OLD TESTAMENT ECONOMY

Concerning the matter of a dispensational transfer, let us consider the case of Peter. On the mount of transfiguration Peter took the lead to propose to the Lord that he build three tabernacles, one for Moses, one for Elijah, and one for the Lord Jesus (Matt. 17:4). "While he was still speaking, behold, a bright cloud overshadowed them, and behold, a voice out of the cloud, saying, This is My beloved Son, in whom I delight; hear Him!" (v. 5). When the disciples heard this, they fell on their face. When they lifted up their eyes, "they saw no one except Jesus Himself alone" (v. 8). Moses and Elijah had disappeared, and only Jesus remained. Peter had proposed to keep Moses and Elijah, that is, the law and the prophets, with Christ, but God took Moses and Elijah away, leaving "no one except Jesus Himself alone." No one except Jesus Himself alone should remain in the New Testament. He is today's Moses, imparting the law of life into His believers, and also today's Elijah, speaking for God and speaking forth God within His believers. This is God's New Testament economy.

In Matthew 17:1-8 we have a clear revelation of the fact that with the coming of Jesus both Moses and Elijah were over. Moses and Elijah represent the entire Old Testament, with Moses representing the law and Elijah representing the prophets. According to Jewish custom, the Old Testament was regarded as having two main parts—the Law and the Prophets. Even the Psalms were considered part of the Law. Therefore, the fact that Moses and Elijah were over indicates that the entire Old Testament, consisting of the Law and the Prophets, was over.

Peter had the experience of seeing the vision on the mount of transfiguration, and later, in his second Epistle, he referred to what happened on that mountain (2 Pet. 1:16-18). Why, then, did Peter say nothing about this vision when James was insisting on keeping the Old Testament economy along with the New Testament economy? I find this difficult to understand. In Acts 21 did Peter not have any remembrance of the vision he had seen in Matthew 17 and about which he later wrote in 2 Peter 1?

Peter certainly was knowledgeable concerning the disappearing of the Old Testament economy. On the mount of transfiguration he must have been impressed with this. He heard the voice out of the cloud declare, "This is My beloved Son, in whom I delight; hear Him!" (Matt. 17:5). He had also seen Moses and Elijah together with Jesus, and then he saw that Moses and Elijah had disappeared and that Jesus remained alone. Why, having heard this word and having seen this vision, was Peter silent in Acts 21? Why did he not rise up and say, "Brother James, let me tell you what I heard and saw on the mount of transfiguration. Moses and Elijah, the Law and the Prophets, are over. We should no longer hold on to the Old Testament economy. To do that is contrary to God's move in His New Testament economy." However,

Peter kept silent and did not speak this way to James in Acts 21. Likewise, there is no indication that John, who was with Peter on the mount of transfiguration, said anything to James concerning it at that juncture. Neither Peter nor John stood up to testify regarding the vision they had seen and the charge they had received on the mount of transfiguration.

THREE EMPHATIC CHARGES

In Matthew 28:19-20a the resurrected Christ said to His disciples, "Go therefore and disciple all the nations, baptizing them into the name of the Father and of the Son and of the Holy Spirit, teaching them to observe all things, whatever I commanded you." "Nations" refers to the Gentiles. The disciples were charged to disciple the Gentiles by baptizing them into the Triune God. The Lord's charge to the disciples in Matthew 28:19 is very emphatic.

According to Mark 16:15, the Lord, after His resurrection and before His ascension, charged the eleven, saying, "Go into all the world and preach the gospel to all the creation." In this verse "creation" mainly denotes different peoples, although it includes more than this. As in Matthew 28:19, here the Lord commands the disciples to preach the gospel to all peoples, to all nations.

After His resurrection and before His ascension, the Lord Jesus spoke yet another word to the disciples to indicate that the gospel should be preached to all nations. In Luke 24:47 He told them that "repentance for forgiveness of sins should be proclaimed in His name to all the nations, beginning from Jerusalem." If we consider these three charges at the end of Matthew, Mark, and Luke, we shall see how strong, definite, emphatic, and absolute they are.

THE SITUATION OF MIXTURE IN JERUSALEM

Regarding the situation of mixture in Jerusalem, Peter and John were silent. There is no record that they did anything to diminish this mixture. Rather, according to Luke's account in Acts, only Paul bore the burden of this matter.

It seems that Peter and John were not concerned about it. If they had been concerned, they should have spoken strongly to James and said, "James, before you were saved, we heard the word and saw the vision about the passing away of the Old Testament economy."

According to the record of the New Testament, the James in Acts 21 was a brother of the Lord Jesus in the flesh. Along with the other brothers of the Lord, James was saved right after His resurrection, if not a little before that time. Therefore, it is possible that James was present when one or more of the charges recorded at the end of Matthew, Mark, and Luke was given. He must have known that the Lord had commanded the disciples to preach the gospel to all the nations.

Why did the disciples, including James, seemingly disregard the Lord's word about preaching the gospel to all the nations and pay so much attention to the Old Testament? Both the revelation given to the disciples and the Lord's charge were clear, definite, emphatic, and absolute. All the disciples, therefore, should have been clear concerning God's economy. But in the midst of the situation in Jerusalem, none of them cared for the Lord's charge. Instead, they were in favor of a mixture of the Old Testament dispensation with God's New Testament economy.

Acts 21:19 says that Paul, after greeting James and all the elders "related one by one the things which God did among the Gentiles through his ministry." When they heard this, they glorified God (v. 20). Then James took the lead to say to Paul, "You observe, brother, how many thousands there are among the Jews who have believed, and all are zealous for the law" (v. 20). It was a shame to James that he spoke such a word. If I had been Peter listening to this word, I would have had a deep sense of shame.

In the early chapters of Acts Peter was bold. He and John were strong when they faced the opposition of the Sanhedrin. However, in chapters fifteen through twenty-one Peter seems to have lost his boldness. According to Paul's word in Galatians 2, Peter even practiced hypocrisy concerning this mixture. How pitiful was the situation in Jerusalem in Acts 21! We all need to be impressed with the picture of this situation. However, we should not blame Peter, for, in principle, we are in the same kind of situation today.

It is correct to say that from the time of Acts 15 Paul was troubled deeply in his spirit about the situation in Jerusalem. Because of his heavy burden concerning this, during the course of his third journey of ministry, he was not able to forget Jerusalem. In 19:21 he purposed in his spirit to go to Jerusalem. His purpose was not only to carry out a loving concern for the need of the poor saints in Jerusalem, but also to have fellowship with James and the others concerning the mixture there. Apparently, Paul purposed to go to Jerusalem in order to bring financial help from the Gentile believers to those in Judea. Actually, in Paul's spirit and heart was the concern for the dreadful situation in Jerusalem, which was the source of the Lord's move on earth. According to Paul's understanding, that source had been polluted. Therefore, he did not have peace to proceed further with the Lord's move. He knew that no matter how much work he accomplished in the Gentile world, the polluted stream from Jerusalem would flow there. Realizing this, Paul purposed in his spirit to return to the source with the intention of trying to clear up the situation, to get rid of the pollution. It was also his desire to go on from there to Rome and even to Spain for the furtherance of the gospel to carry out God's New Testament economy.

THE LORD'S INTOLERANCE, SOVEREIGNTY, AND SYMPATHY

It seems that when Paul went to Jerusalem the last time, he did not have the opportunity to help matters there. Rather, the door was firmly closed, and he was pressed by James and the elders into a very difficult situation. Having no way out, he acted on the proposal to go to the temple in order to be purified with the four who had a Nazarite vow. But, as we have seen, the Lord did not tolerate this.

In 21:23 and 24 James said to Paul, "Four men are with us who have a vow on themselves; take these and be purified with them, and pay their expenses that they may shave their heads; and all will know that there is nothing to the things of which they have been instructed concerning you, but that you yourself also walk orderly, keeping the law." We have seen that the vow in verse 23 was the Nazarite vow (Num. 6:2-5) and that to be purified with the Nazarites was to become a Nazarite with them and to join with them in their vow.

Acts 21:26 goes on to say, "Then Paul took the men on the following day, and having been purified with them entered into the temple, giving notice of the completion of the days of the purification, until the offering was offered for each one of them." This was an extremely serious matter. A Nazarite vow was not something ordinary; rather, it was special, particular, and extraordinary. Furthermore, the offerings related to the Nazarite vow were particular. It is difficult to believe, therefore, that the apostle Paul would go back to the temple, participate in the Nazarite vow, and wait for the priests to offer sacrifices for him and the others.

According to what Paul had written in the Epistles to the Romans and the Galatians, he should not have returned to the temple, and he certainly should not have participated in this vow. It is no surprise, then, that the Lord did not tolerate this situation. Paul may have been trying to keep the peace, but the Lord allowed a great uproar to take place against Paul.

It was a very serious matter for an apostle such as Paul, after writing the Epistles to the Romans and the Galatians, to join himself with those who had the Nazarite vow and go with them to the temple to be purified and then to remain in the temple until the priest came to offer the sacrifices. The Lord tolerated Paul's private vow in 18:18, but He did not tolerate Paul's joining himself to those with the Nazarite vow in chapter twenty-one.

Actually, Paul should not even have made the vow in chapter eighteen. In Galatians 2:20 he had declared that he had been crucified with Christ. There Paul seemed to be saying, "I, the Jewish Paul, have been crucified with Christ. Now it is no longer I who live, but Christ lives in me." However, in having a vow in the Jewish way, Paul was living not as a Christian but as a Jew, for he was following a Jewish practice, not a Christian one.

All the believers in Jerusalem were Jews. It was in Antioch that the believers were first called Christians (11:26). Had Paul forgotten the term "Christian" when, in Acts 18, he was carrying out a Jewish practice? Should a Christian have a vow for thanksgiving in a Jewish way? If not, then why did Paul continue to practice something Jewish? Although the Lord tolerated that practice, He had no toleration for what was taking place in Acts 21, when Paul was awaiting the time for the priests to offer the sacrifices at the completion of the days of purification.

From 21:27 onward we see the Lord's sovereignty in a particular way. We also see His sympathy. On the one hand, Paul was faithful. He was even willing to risk his life for the Lord's name (20:24; 21:13). He was ready "to die in Jerusalem for the name of the Lord Jesus" (21:13). On the other hand, Paul was still human and was not able to help himself in Acts 21. The Lord did not have anyone better or more faithful than Paul. Therefore, He intervened first to rescue Paul from the mixture in Jerusalem and then from the Jews who were plotting to kill him. Eventually, he was placed in Roman custody, separated from troubles and disturbances. In this way the Lord gave Paul a tranquil time for the writing of his last Epistles. In particular, Paul was given the opportunity to write the four crucial Epistles of Hebrews, Ephesians, Philippians, and Colossians. Let us now briefly consider these four Epistles, which should be grouped together.

FOUR CRUCIAL EPISTLES

Hebrews

In Hebrews we see that Christ is far superior to everything in Judaism. In Judaism there is God. According to Hebrews 1, Christ is the very God. Furthermore, in Hebrews 2 we see that Christ is also man. The God in Judaism is merely God, but the God in the New Testament is both God and man, the God-man. As such a God-man, Christ is superior to the angels, another important item of Judaism. Furthermore, the book of Hebrews reveals that Christ is superior to Moses, Joshua, and Aaron, the priest.

According to the book of Hebrews, the new covenant enacted by Christ is superior to the old covenant enacted by Moses (8:6-13), and Christ's unique sacrifice is superior to the old sacrifices (10:9-10, 12, 14). God now cares only for Christ's unique sacrifice, which has terminated and replaced all the Old Testament sacrifices.

In the book of Hebrews Paul presents a clear picture showing us that the Old Testament things are over. What remains now in God's New Testament economy is Jesus Christ, the all-inclusive One. Having seen such a view, Paul could not tolerate a mixture of such an all-inclusive Christ with the inferior things of the out-of-date, Old Testament economy.

Ephesians

In the book of Ephesians Paul indicates that all the believers, both Jews and Gentiles, need a spirit of wisdom and revelation to see God's calling, which issues in the church, Christ's Body, the fullness of the One who fills all in all (1:17-23). In Ephesians 2 Paul goes on to point out that all the ordinances in the Old Testament law have been abolished through Christ's death on the cross so that in Christ the Jews and the Gentiles might be created into one new man (vv. 14-16). In chapter three we see that the riches of Christ need to become the constituent of the church life, and that we need Christ to make His home in our hearts so that we may be filled unto all the fullness of the Triune God to become His full expression (vv. 8, 17-19). In chapter four Paul speaks of the one Body, the one Spirit, the one Lord, and the one God (vv. 4-6). The Body is constituted of and mingled with the Triune God to become the new man (v. 24). Following this, in chapter five Paul indicates that the new man should be filled in the spirit with the Triune God in order to have a life that is the expression of the Triune God in Christ (v. 18). Finally, in Ephesians 6 we see that we must fight a spiritual battle for the kingdom of God (v. 11). This is a brief summary of the revelation in Ephesians.

Philippians

In Philippians 3:7 Paul says, "What things were gains to me, these I have counted loss on account of Christ." Paul was a Hebrew of the Hebrews, a Pharisee as to the law (3:5). However, he counted all Jewish things, all the things of the Old Testament, as dung in order that he might gain Christ (3:8). Paul knew that in God's New Testament economy Christ must be everything. Therefore, Paul pursued Christ so that he might live a life of being found in Christ (3:9-14).

Colossians

According to the revelation in the book of Colossians, Christ is the reality of every positive thing. Christ is the portion God has given to the saints (1:12), the image of God (v. 15), the Firstborn of all creation (v. 15), the Firstborn from among the dead (v. 18), the mystery of God (2:2), the embodiment of the Godhead (2:9), our feast, new moon, and Sabbath (2:16-17), and our life (Col. 3:4). In Colossians we see that Christ must be everything to us. Colossians also says clearly that in the new man, composed of all the believers, there cannot be Greek and Jew, circumcision and uncircumcision, but Christ is all and in all.

If we consider together Hebrews, Ephesians, Philippians, and Colossians, we shall see that to such an enlightened one as Paul, in God's New Testament economy there is nothing but Christ. However, what Paul saw in Jerusalem during his last visit there was a mixture. Something of Christ was mixed with the things of the Old Testament economy.

COMING BACK TO CHRIST
AS OUR TREE OF LIFE, MANNA, AND FEAST

Through Paul's completing ministry (Col. 1:25) the all-inclusive Christ is revealed in a full way. In the fourteen

Epistles of Paul, especially in Hebrews, Ephesians, Philippians, and Colossians, Christ is unveiled as everything to the church and to the saints. But by the time the book of Revelation was written this view of the all-inclusive Christ had been all but lost. This loss is indicated by the seven epistles in Revelation 2 and 3. Christ, the Head of the Body, came in to call the overcomers to overcome the degraded situation. The overcomers in Revelation do not simply overcome sin, the world, and the flesh; they especially overcome the degraded situation in which the clear view of the all-inclusive Christ has been lost.

In Revelation 2:7 the Lord Jesus says, "To him who overcomes, to him I will give to eat of the tree of life, which is in the paradise of God." In 2:17 He goes on to say, "To him who overcomes, to him I will give of the hidden manna, and I will give him a white stone, and on the stone a new name written, which no one knows but he who receives it." Furthermore, in 3:20 the Lord says, "Behold, I stand at the door and knock; if anyone hears My voice and opens the door, I will come in to him and dine with him and he with Me." These verses speak of the tree of life, the hidden manna, and feasting with the Lord. Here the Lord seems to be saying, "You need to enjoy Me and forget outward practices and forms. Come back directly to Me as your tree of life, manna, and feast. Turn from all the mixtures and the things replacing Me in the degraded churches and come back to Me as your everything."

The problem in today's degraded situation is that many things are replacing the all-inclusive Christ. We need to turn from all replacements and come back directly to the all-inclusive Christ as our tree of life, our hidden manna, our feast, and our everything. We need to come back to this One in the way of enjoyment, not merely in the way of doctrine. We need to return to Him not only in the way of knowing Him objectively, but in the way of enjoying Him as the tree of life, the hidden manna, and the feast.

To overcome the degraded situation among today's Christians and to come back directly to the enjoyable Christ as our tree of life, hidden manna, and feast is to have a real transfer. This is a transfer out of old degraded religion into an up-to-date recovery, a recovery of the enjoyment of the all-inclusive Christ. Today this Christ is not only the life-giving Spirit (1 Cor. 15:45)—He is the sevenfold, intensified Spirit (Rev. 5:6).

We need to have an overall view to see today's degraded situation and also to see that the Lord's intention is to bring us back to Himself so that we may be fully recovered to the enjoyment of Him. Every day we should know only one thing—to enjoy Christ as the tree of life, the hidden manna, and the feast. We need to enjoy Christ as our everything, even as our white garments (Rev. 3:5) and the white stone (2:17) to make us building materials for God's eternal habitation. Our need today is to experience a transfer from degraded religion to the reality of the all-inclusive Christ in the way of enjoyment.

LIFE-STUDY OF ACTS

MESSAGE SIXTY

THE PROPAGATION
IN ASIA MINOR AND EUROPE
THROUGH THE MINISTRY OF PAUL'S COMPANY

(26)

Scripture Reading: Acts 21:27—22:29

Acts 21:27—26:32 is a lengthy section that records the ultimate persecution by the Jews. In 21:27—23:15 we have an account of an uproar against Paul. In this message we shall see that Paul was seized by the Jews in Jerusalem (21:27-30), that the Roman commander intervened (21:31-39), and that Paul was given the opportunity to defend himself before the rioting Jews (21:40—22:21). After making his defense, Paul was bound by the Romans (22:22-29).

SEIZED BY THE JEWS IN JERUSALEM

Acts 21:27 and 28 say, "Now when the seven days were about to be concluded, the Jews from Asia saw him in the temple and threw all the crowd into confusion; and they laid their hands on him, crying out, Men, Israelites, help! This is the man who is teaching all men everywhere against the people, and the law, and this place; and besides, he has even brought Greeks into the temple and has profaned this holy place." Yes, God's New Testament teaching according to His New Testament economy is really against the Jews who oppose God's New Testament economy (Matt. 21:41, 43-45; 22:7; 23:32-36; Acts 7:51; 13:40-41), against the law of dead letters (Rom. 3:20, 28; 6:14; 7:4, 6; Gal. 2:19, 21; 5:4), and against the holy place, the temple (Matt. 23:38; 24:2; Acts 7:48). Because Paul's ministry was to carry out God's New Testament economy, it could not please the Jews who were possessed and usurped by Satan, the enemy of God, with their deformed traditional religion, to oppose and ravage God's New Testament move. Rather, it offended them and it stirred up their jealousy and hatred to the uttermost, so that they made a plot (20:3) to do away with him (21:31, 36).

In 21:28 "this place" and "this holy place" refer to the temple. Verses 29 and 30 continue, "For they had previously seen Trophimus the Ephesian in the city with him, whom they supposed Paul had brought into the temple. And the whole city was aroused, and the people ran together; and laying hold of Paul, they dragged him outside the temple; and immediately the doors were shut." Literally, the Greek words translated "the people ran together" mean "a running together of the people occurred."

THE INTERVENTION OF THE ROMAN COMMANDER

Acts 21:31-33 says, "And as they were seeking to kill him, a report came up to the commander of the cohort that all Jerusalem was in confusion. And he took soldiers and centurions at once and ran down to them; and when they saw the commander and the soldiers, they ceased beating Paul. Then the commander drew near and laid hold of him and ordered him to be bound with two chains, and he inquired who he might be and what he had done." This commander was a chiliarch in command of a thousand troops, or a cohort. A cohort was one of the ten divisions of an ancient Roman legion. In His sovereignty, the Lord used the intervention of this Roman commander to rescue Paul from the Jews, who were seeking to kill him.

DEFENDING HIMSELF BEFORE THE RIOTING JEWS

Paul's Need to Make a Defense

Paul asked permission of the Roman commander to speak to the people (v. 39). When the commander had given him permission, Paul addressed the people in the Hebrew dialect. This dialect was Aramaic, the language then spoken in Palestine.

In 22:1 Paul said, "Men, brothers, and fathers, hear my defense which I now make to you." Paul faced his opponents in a way different from Christ. Christ was a lamb brought to the slaughter, and as a sheep dumb before its shearer for the accomplishment of His redemption, He did not open His mouth when judged by men (Isa. 53:7; Matt. 26:62-63; 27:12, 14). But Paul, a faithful and bold apostle sent by the Lord, needed to make a defense and to exercise his wisdom to save his life from his persecutors so that he might fulfill the course of his ministry. Although he was willing and ready to sacrifice his life for the Lord (20:24; 21:13), he still endeavored to live longer that he might carry out the Lord's ministry as much as possible.

Persecuting This Way

In 22:3 and 4 Paul went on to say, "I am a man who is a Jew, born in Tarsus of Cilicia, but brought up in this city at the feet of Gamaliel, having been trained according to the strictness of the law of our fathers, being zealous for God, even as you all are today. And I persecuted this way unto death, binding and delivering to prisons both men and women." As we have seen, "this way" denotes the way of the Lord's full salvation in God's New Testament economy.

In verse 5 Paul continued by saying that the high priest and all the council of the elders could testify for him. The Greek word for "council" here is *presbuterion,* presbytery, eldership (of the Sanhedrin), hence the Sanhedrin, the highest court of the Jews composed of the chief priests, elders, lawyers, and scribes.

Paul's Experience on the Road to Damascus

In 22:6 and 7 Paul says, "Now it came about that as I was journeying and drawing near to Damascus, about midday, suddenly a great light shone out of heaven around me, and I fell to the ground and heard a voice saying to me, Saul, Saul, why are you persecuting Me?" Literally, the Greek word for "great" in verse 6 means considerable. As we have pointed out, the "Me" in verse 7 was a corporate Me, including Jesus the Lord and all His believers, all the members of His Body. From that time he began to see that the Lord Jesus and His believers are one great person, a wonderful "Me."

Verse 8 continues, "And I answered, Who are You, Lord? And He said to me, I am Jesus the Nazarene, whom you are persecuting." Even without knowing the Lord Jesus, Paul called Him Lord. Then the Lord indicated that Paul, by persecuting His followers, who were united to Him through their faith in Him, was actually persecuting Him.

In verse 9 Paul says, "And those who were with me beheld the light, but did not hear the voice of the One who was speaking to me." To say that they did not hear the voice means that they did not hear in the sense of understanding, as in Mark 4:33 and 1 Corinthians 14:2. They heard the voice (Acts 9:7), but they did not understand it, just as they beheld the light, but beheld no one.

According to verse 10, Paul went on to say, "What shall I do, Lord? And the Lord said to me, Rise up and go into Damascus, and there it will be told you concerning all things which have been appointed for you to do." Here we see that the Lord would not directly tell Paul right after his conversion what He wanted him to do, for the reason that He needed a member of His Body to initiate him into the identification with His Body.

Acts 22:11 says, "And as I could not see because of the glory of that light, I was led by the hand of those who were with me and came into Damascus." This was the Lord's dealing with Paul who, prior to his conversion, considered himself knowledgeable concerning man and God.

Initiated into the Identification with the Body of Christ

Verses 12 and 13 continue, "And a certain Ananias, a devout man according to the law, well attested by all the Jews dwelling there, came to me, and standing by said to me, Saul, brother, receive your sight! And in that very hour I looked up at him." We know from 9:11-17 that the Lord sent Ananias, one member of His Body, to Paul so that he might be initiated into the identification with His Body. This must have impressed him with the importance of the Body of Christ and helped him realize that a believer needs the members of the Body of Christ.

According to 22:14-16 Ananias said to Paul, "The God of our fathers has appointed you to know His will, and to see the Righteous One, and to hear the voice of His mouth; for you will be a witness to Him unto all men of the things which you have seen and heard. And now, why do you delay? Rise up and be baptized, and wash away your sins, calling on His name." "His" is significant here. It points particularly to the name of the One whom Paul hated and persecuted (v. 8).

The Greek word translated "calling on" is *epikaleo*. This word is composed of *epi,* upon, and *kaleo,* call by name; that is, to call out audibly, even loudly, as Stephen did in 7:59-60.

Calling on the Lord's name in 22:16 was a means for Paul to wash away his sins in arresting so many of the believers who called on the Lord's name. All the believers knew that he considered calling on the Lord's name a sign of those he should arrest (9:14, 21). Now he had turned unto the Lord. In order to wash away his sins in persecuting and arresting the Lord's callers, not only before God but also before all the believers, Ananias charged him to do the same calling, which he had condemned, at his baptism, a public confession of the Lord whom he had persecuted.

Sent to the Gentiles

In 22:17 and 18 Paul goes on to say, "And it came about that when I returned to Jerusalem and was praying in the temple, I came into a trance, and I saw Him saying to me, Hurry, and go quickly out of Jerusalem, because they will not accept your testimony concerning Me." The Greek word rendered "trance" is *ekstasis,* and may be translated "ecstasy." This Greek word means being put out of its place; hence, it refers to a state in which a man passes out of himself and from which he comes to himself (12:11), as in a dream, but without sleep. It differs from a vision, in which definite objects are visible.

In 22:19 and 20 Paul said to the Lord, "Lord, they know that I was imprisoning and beating in every synagogue those who believe on You, and when the blood of Your witness Stephen was being shed, I myself also was standing by and consenting and keeping the garments of those who did away with him." Nevertheless, the Lord said to him, "Go, for I will send you to Gentiles afar off" (v. 21). We are told the people "listened to him up to this word" (v. 22). But hearing the word "Gentiles," they began to shout, "Away with such a man from the earth, for it is not fitting for him to live!" (v. 22). Actually, the word "Gentiles" uttered by Paul in verse 21 is related to the matter of the dispensational transfer. As soon as he spoke this word, it seems that a whirlwind came to stir up the people. They were provoked by this word and were not willing to listen any longer.

In Acts 22 Paul was somewhat cautious in presenting his experience on the way to Damascus. Yet he could not avoid relating a particular aspect of the truth—the Lord's word to go to the Gentiles afar off. Since the Lord had told him this, how could he not testify of it to the people? They, however, did not have the ears to hear such a word. The principle is the same among many Christians today. Just as the Jews in Acts 22 did not want to hear anything about the Gentiles, so these Christians do not want to hear us speak concerning the denominations, the church, the church ground, and Christ being the life-giving Spirit. From experience we know that if we talk to certain believers about these matters, they will be offended.

BOUND BY THE ROMANS

Acts 22:23 and 24 say, "And as they were crying out and throwing off their garments and throwing dust in the air, the commander ordered him to be brought into the barracks, saying that he should be examined by scourging in order that he might ascertain for what cause they were shouting against him so." But as they stretched out Paul with the thongs, he said to a centurion standing by, "Is it lawful for you to scourge a man who is a Roman and uncondemned?"

(v. 25). Here we see Paul's wisdom. He utilized his Roman citizenship to save himself from suffering persecution.

In these chapters in Acts we see that the Lord's sovereign hand surely was with Paul. In His sovereignty, wisdom, and goodness the Lord rescued Paul and protected him. In chapter twenty-one Paul was forced into a very difficult situation, and he had no way to be released from it. The Lord, however, raised up the environment through which Paul was rescued from that situation. However, Paul was then in danger of being killed. But the Lord intervened through the Roman commander to protect Paul from the Jews who wanted to kill him.

As we shall see, after Paul was placed in Roman custody, "the Jews formed a plot and put themselves under a curse, saying that they would neither eat nor drink until they had killed Paul. Now there were more than forty who formed this conspiracy" (23:12-13). However, the son of Paul's sister heard of the ambush and reported it to Paul (23:16). Paul then called one of the centurions and told him to bring the young man to the commander. When the commander heard of the plot, he said to two of the centurions, "Prepare two hundred soldiers that they may go as far as Caesarea, and seventy horsemen, and two hundred spearmen by the third hour of the night, and mounts to stand by to put Paul on that they may bring him safely to Felix the governor" (23:23-24). We may be surprised that so many soldiers, horsemen, and spearmen were involved in transferring Paul from Jerusalem to Caesarea. The commander may have ordered this because of the large number of Jews involved in the uproar against Paul. The point we are making concerning this is that here we see the Lord's sovereign protection of Paul.

In Caesarea Paul was kept in custody for two years. During these years he was safely guarded, protected from the plotting Jews. This became a golden time for Paul to consider his future. In particular, it was a time for him to consider the matters he would later put into writing in such books as Hebrews, Ephesians, Philippians, and Colossians.

Sovereignly the Lord prepared an environment to safeguard Paul and to prepare him to carry out his writing ministry to complete his ministry and to complete the New Testament revelation.

LIFE-STUDY OF ACTS

MESSAGE SIXTY-ONE

THE PROPAGATION
IN ASIA MINOR AND EUROPE
THROUGH THE MINISTRY OF PAUL'S COMPANY

(27)

Scripture Reading: Acts 22:1-21

PAUL'S BAPTISM

In 22:1-21 Paul defends himself before the rioting Jews. In this message we shall focus our attention on Ananias' word to Paul in verse 16: "And now, why do you delay? Rise up and be baptized, and wash away your sins, calling on His name."

In the case of Paul, like that of the Ethiopian eunuch, water baptism is emphasized. We need to pay attention both to water baptism and Spirit baptism. Water baptism signifies the believers' identification with Christ's death and resurrection (Rom. 6:3-5; Col. 2:12), and Spirit baptism signifies the reality of the believers' union with Christ in life essentially and in power economically. Water baptism is the believers' affirmation of the Spirit's reality. Both are needed, and neither can replace the other. All believers in Christ should properly have both.

According to the Lord's word in Mark 16:16, in order to be saved, a person must believe and be baptized. To believe is to receive the Lord (John 1:12) not only for forgiveness of sins (Acts 10:43), but also for regeneration (1 Pet. 1:21, 23), so that those who believe may become the children of God (John 1:12-13) and the members of Christ (Eph. 5:30) in an organic union with the Triune God (Matt. 28:19). To be baptized is to affirm this by being buried to terminate the old creation through Christ's death and by being raised up to be a new creation of God through Christ's resurrection. Such a baptism is much more advanced than the baptism of repentance by John (Mark 1:4; Acts 19:3-5).

To believe and to be baptized are two parts of one complete step for receiving the full salvation of God. To be baptized without believing is merely an empty ritual; to believe without being baptized is to be saved only inwardly without an outward affirmation of the inward salvation. These two should go together.

TRANSFERRED OUT OF ADAM INTO CHRIST

Baptism is actually a great transfer. For this reason, the New Testament ministry began with baptism. We have emphasized the fact that baptism involves first termination and then germination. Through termination and germination a real transfer takes place. It is not surprising, then, that the New Testament begins with baptism to indicate that the things of the Old Testament should be terminated in order to have a new beginning. However, among many Christians today, baptism is simply a ritual whereby people enter into another kind of religion.

When we were baptized, we were transferred out of Adam into Christ. Many Christians have never been taught this adequately. Others know that in baptism they were transferred out of Adam into Christ, but for them this is only a doctrinal matter. It is not something practical in their Christian life. In our living as Christians we should be out of Adam and in Christ. No longer should we live in the sphere of Adam; instead, our living should absolutely be in the sphere of Christ.

CALLING ON THE NAME OF THE LORD

In 22:16 Ananias told Paul to be baptized and wash away his sins, calling on the name of the Lord. In this verse "calling on His name" modifies both "be baptized" and "wash." Here Ananias seems to be saying, "Paul, rise up and be baptized. As you are being baptized, you must call on the name of the Lord. Calling on His name is the condition of your being baptized."

It would be a good practice for us when baptizing new believers to charge them to call on the name of the Lord Jesus. This means that while they are being baptized, they are calling on the name of the Lord. Just as we breathe and eat at the same time, so a person may be baptized and call on the Lord at the same time. The transfer that takes place through baptism is strengthened by one's calling on the Lord's name. Therefore, let us charge those who are being baptized by us to call on the name of the Lord Jesus and thereby have a stronger transfer out of Adam into Christ.

A Condition for Baptism
and for the Washing Away of Sins

In 22:16 Ananias told Paul to rise up, be baptized, and wash away his sins. We have seen that "calling on His name" modifies both "be baptized" and "wash." Calling is a condition both of being baptized and of washing away sins. Calling on the Lord's name was a means for Paul to wash away his sins.

According to Ananias' understanding, what were Paul's sins that needed to be washed away? No doubt, the most serious sins, according to Ananias, were the sins of persecuting and arresting those who called on the name of Jesus. Paul's going out to arrest those who called on the Lord's name was his major sin. In this matter he was condemned not only by God but also by the believers, both in Jerusalem and elsewhere. All the believers condemned Paul as a persecutor. Paul regarded the calling on the name of the Lord as a sign of the believers. Therefore, wherever Paul went, he sought out those who called on the Lord's name.

In 22:16 Ananias seemed to be saying, "Paul, in the eyes of the believers your most serious sin was persecuting and arresting those who called on the Lord. Now that you have repented and have had a turn, you need to wash away your sins. In particular, you need to wash away the sin of persecuting the saints. In order to wash away your sins, you need to call on the name of the Lord. If you call, 'O Lord Jesus,' a number of times, the saints will forgive you. Your calling will be the condition for the washing away of your sins. Paul, you cannot be a silent believer, a believer who does not audibly call on the Lord's name. If you are silent, the believers will not recognize you as one of them, and they will not forgive you. Therefore, you must now practice the very thing that you condemned—calling on the name of the Lord Jesus. Once you took this as a sign of those to be persecuted and arrested by you. Now it should be a sign that you have believed in the Lord Jesus and have been saved. Paul, rise up, be baptized, and wash away your sins, calling on His name. When you do this, you will be forgiven by all those who love the Lord Jesus."

The Initial Step of Paul's Transfer

Paul's calling on the name of the Lord Jesus was the initial step of his transfer. He was transferred from condemning this calling to practicing it. Some may say that calling on the Lord's name was a part of Paul's conversion. Yes, but that was not only part of his conversion; it was also the beginning of his transfer from one realm into another.

It is difficult to understand why the Jews opposed the matter of calling on the Lord's name. To the Jews the important matters were keeping the law and practicing circumcision and following the customs. Nevertheless, before his transfer, Paul particularly opposed the calling on the Lord's name.

The principle is the same today among those who oppose the practice of calling on the name of the Lord Jesus. Some condemn us for calling on the name of the Lord. Actually, they have no reason to oppose this practice. Nevertheless, some falsely say that it is mere shouting. But what is wrong with believers in the Lord calling on His name? This practice is strongly revealed in the Scriptures. It is better to call on the Lord's name than to be silent, dead, and without any genuine contact with the Lord.

Some who oppose calling on the name of the Lord Jesus say, "Christianity has been on earth for nineteen hundred years, but we have never heard this teaching that believers should call on the Lord's name." To this we may reply,

"Perhaps you have never heard this kind of teaching, but certainly you have heard believers call on the Lord's name. In fact, it is likely that in the years you have been a Christian you have had at least some experience of calling on the name of Jesus yourself."

There have been many cases of those who called on the Lord's name without receiving any teaching concerning this practice. One particular person strongly opposed our calling on the Lord's name. One day as he was riding his bicycle, he was hit by a car, and the bicycle was thrown into the air. While he was falling to the ground, he spontaneously called, "O Lord Jesus!"

I also know of a certain Christian husband who never prayed. One day his wife was involved in an accident. Do you know what he did? He called on the name of the Lord.

Do you know of any genuine Christian who can say that he has never called on the name of the Lord Jesus? Certainly every real believer in Christ has called upon His name at some time. That brother who was hit by a car while riding a bicycle spent some days in the hospital, and day by day he called, "O Lord Jesus." No one taught him to call; he called automatically. Many of us can testify that when we call on the Lord Jesus, we truly contact Him.

Have you ever had the experience of falling asleep when you were trying to pray? This happened to me a number of times as I was praying silently, especially late at night. From experience we know that silent prayer often puts us to sleep. Furthermore, with that kind of prayer there may be little enjoyment of the Lord, if any. However, when we call on the name of the Lord, we enjoy Him. We may call quietly in order not to disturb others, but we still enjoy the Lord by calling on His name.

A Necessity in Our Christian Life

I am concerned about those who are troubled by our emphasis on calling on the name of the Lord Jesus. It is not correct to say that we stress this too much. Actually, calling on the Lord is a necessity in our Christian life. If you practice calling on the Lord's name, you will be in the initial stage of the dispensational transfer. I assure you that the more you call on the name of the Lord Jesus, the more you will be brought out of the old things into the new.

Some believers have been Christians for many years. As the years have gone by, their Christian life has become quite old. Because of this oldness, they need to experience a transfer in a practical way. The most prevailing way to have such a transfer is to call, "O Lord Jesus!" I encourage you to practice this. If you call on the Lord's name day by day, you will be able to testify many things concerning your experience of the Lord.

Calling on the name of the Lord is a great help to Christian husbands. Married brothers often have difficulty in loving their wives. If a married brother will call on the name of the Lord Jesus, he will experience a genuine change in relation to his wife and truly love her.

Likewise, a married sister can be helped by calling on the Lord's name to submit to her husband. If such a sister does not contact the Lord by calling on Him, she may say to herself, "It is not fair that I must submit to my husband. Why should I submit to him? God is not fair to ordain that he be the head instead of me." God's word, however, cannot be changed. Neither can this married sister ignore the requirement that she should submit to her husband. How, then, can she be helped? The best way for her to receive help in the matter of submitting to her husband is to call on the Lord's name. If she calls on Him day by day, she will be able to submit to her husband.

When we call on the Lord's name, we experience a real transfer. We are brought into another realm; we are brought into the kingdom of God, which is actually the propagated Christ Himself. If we realize this, we shall understand why the matter of calling on the name of the Lord is emphasized so much in the Bible.

Whenever we call on the Lord, He has both the opportunity and ground to spread Himself within us. This is not a mere doctrine; it is something very practical for our Christian experience. Today our Lord is the all-inclusive Spirit. As the Spirit, He is omnipresent, and He is now working within us, waiting for the opportunity to spread in us. When we call on His name, we give Him the way to increase in us.

To Participate in the Lord's Riches

An important verse related to calling on the Lord is Romans 10:12: "There is no difference between Jew and Greek; for the same Lord of all is rich to all who call upon Him." For years, I knew only the following verse in Romans 10: "Whoever calls upon the name of the Lord shall be saved" (v. 13). I had been told that whoever calls on the name of the Lord will be saved, but I had never heard that the Lord is rich to all who call on His name. He is rich not only in initial salvation—He is rich in all divine and spiritual things. If we would participate in the Lord's riches, we need to call on Him. Day and night, we should call on the name of the Lord. Although we may call quietly so as not to disturb others, we can still softly call, "O Lord Jesus."

To Be Brought into Our Spirit

Once we call on the Lord's name, we cannot remain in our natural thoughts and reasonings. From experience we know that when we call on the name of the Lord we are brought into the depths of our being, that is, we are brought into our spirit. We cannot call on the name of the Lord and at the same time stay in the natural mind. Those who reason concerning the calling may say, "Is it right to call on the name of the Lord? Is this practice scriptural? If it is scriptural, why has it not been taught by others during the last nineteen centuries?" If such a person will call on the Lord, he will be saved from his natural thoughts and reasonings. When we refuse to call we remain in the natural mind. But when we call on the Lord, we are brought into the spirit. Oh, how we need to call on the Lord so that we may enjoy Him!

To Experience the Lord's Nearness

Calling on the Lord is a reality, for when we call on Him we touch Him. In a verse related to this calling Paul says: "The word is near you, in your mouth" (Rom. 10:8). In a very practical sense, the word here is equal to the Lord. Thus, for the word to be near means that the Lord is near. Whenever we call on the name of the Lord, we experience His nearness, His intimate presence.

How do we know that the Lord is near us? We know this by calling on the Lord. You cannot convince someone that the Lord is near him by arguing or debating with him. The more we argue, the farther away the Lord may seem to be. But if instead of arguing we call on His name a few times, we shall sense that He is near. If we continue calling on Him, we shall realize that He is not only near but even within us. The more we call on the Lord, the more He becomes our enjoyment. Through calling on Him He also becomes our peace, rest, comfort, and solution in all kinds of situations. This is not a mere doctrine or superficial teaching; this is a truth for our experience.

REMAINING IN THE TRANSFER
BY BEING FAITHFUL TO OUR VISION

With Paul, we all should learn to call on the name of the Lord Jesus in order to have a complete transfer. Then, also with Paul, we should be faithful to our vision. As we shall see, Paul was able to testify, "I was not disobedient to the heavenly vision" (26:19). Paul's faithfulness is seen in his not avoiding the use of the word "Gentiles" in 22:21. May we all learn to be faithful to the vision we have seen concerning the church, the ground of the church, and Christ as the life-giving Spirit.

We should learn of Paul to present the truth in a very good way. However, this does not mean that we shall always be able to avoid opposition and attack. No matter what our presentation of the truth may be, certain ones will still oppose. Nevertheless, we must be faithful. If at any time we are not faithful to the Lord's vision, then we are no longer in the dispensational transfer. The way to keep ourselves in this transfer is to be faithful. First, we make the transfer by calling on the name of the Lord. Then we remain in this transfer by being faithful to our vision.

LIFE-STUDY OF ACTS

MESSAGE SIXTY-TWO

THE PROPAGATION
IN ASIA MINOR AND EUROPE
THROUGH THE MINISTRY OF PAUL'S COMPANY

(28)

Scripture Reading: Acts 22:30—23:35

DEFENDING HIMSELF BEFORE THE SANHEDRIN

We have seen that in 21:31-39 the Roman commander intervened to rescue Paul from the Jews who were seeking to kill him. Paul was then given the opportunity to defend himself before the rioting Jews (21:40—22:21). The Jews listened to him up to a point, but eventually began to make a disturbance. Paul was then bound by the Romans (22:22-29). In his wisdom, Paul utilized his Roman citizenship to save himself from suffering persecution (vv. 25-29). The Roman commander then gave Paul the opportunity to defend himself before the Sanhedrin (22:30—23:10). Acts 22:30 says, "And on the next day, intending to know for certain why he was accused by the Jews, he released him and ordered the chief priests and all the Sanhedrin to come together; and having brought Paul down, he had him stand before them." Let us now consider Paul's defense given before the Sanhedrin.

Conducting Himself in All Good Conscience

Acts 23:1 says, "And Paul, looking intently at the Sanhedrin, said. Men, brothers, I have conducted myself in all good conscience before God until this day." Following man's fall and his being sent out of the garden of Eden (Gen. 3:23), God wanted man, in His dispensation, to be responsible to his own conscience. But man failed to live and walk according to

his conscience and fell further into wickedness (Gen. 6:5).
After the judgment of the flood, God ordained man to be
under human government (Gen. 9:6). Man failed also in this.
Then, before fulfilling His promise to Abraham concerning
the blessing of the nations in Christ (Gen. 12:3; Gal. 3:8),
God put man under the test of the law (Rom. 3:20; 5:20).
Man failed utterly in this test. All these failures indicate
that man has fallen from God to his conscience, from his
conscience to human government, and from human government to lawlessness. Therefore, man has fallen to the
uttermost.

To conduct oneself "in all good conscience before God," as
Paul did, was a great return to God from man's fall. Paul
spoke this word to vindicate himself before those who
accused him of being a lawless and even reckless person. He
referred, in his defense, to his conscience again in 24:16.
This showed his high standard of morality in contrast to the
hypocrisy of the Jewish religionists and the crookedness of
the Roman (Gentile) politicians.

In his defense before the Sanhedrin in the presence of
representatives of the Roman government, Paul could say
that there was nothing wrong in his personal conduct. He
did all things according to his conscience, behaving in the
highest standard of morality.

Paul's Boldness and Wisdom

Acts 23:2 and 3 continue, "And the high priest Ananias
commanded those who stood by him to strike him on the
mouth. Then Paul said to him, God is going to strike you,
you whitewashed wall! And you sit, judging me according to
the law, and contrary to the law you order me to be struck?"
Here we see Paul's straightforwardness and boldness in
dealing with his persecutors. Those standing by said to him,
"Do you revile the high priest of God?" (v. 4). Paul replied,
"I did not know, brothers, that he is the high priest; for it is
written, You shall not speak evilly of a ruler of your people"
(v. 5).

Acts 23:6 says, "And Paul, knowing that one part was

Sadducees, but the other Pharisees, cried out in the Sanhedrin, Men, brothers, I am a Pharisee, a son of Pharisees;
concerning the hope and resurrection of the dead I am being
judged!" The Pharisees were the strictest religious sect of
the Jews (26:5), formed about 200 B.C. They were proud of
their superior sanctity of life, devotion to God, and knowledge of the Scriptures. Actually, they were degraded into
pretentious conduct and hypocrisy (Matt. 23:2-33). The Sadducees were another sect among Judaism. They did not
believe in the resurrection, nor in angels, nor in spirits.
While the Pharisees were supposed to be orthodox, the
Sadducees were ancient modernists.

When Paul declared that he was a Pharisee and that he
was being judged concerning the hope and resurrection of
the dead, "a dissension arose between the Pharisees and
Sadducees; and the multitude was divided. For the Sadducees say that there is no resurrection, neither angel nor
spirit; but the Pharisees acknowledge both. And there was a
great outcry; and some of the scribes of the Pharisees' party
rose up and fought it out, saying, We find nothing evil in this
man; and if a spirit has spoken to him, or an angel..."
(vv. 7-9). Paul wisely used this situation to his benefit,
knowing that the Pharisees would take sides with him and
then fight with the Sadducees.

When Paul realized that it was helpful to him to take his
stand as a Roman citizen, he did so, and this frightened the
Roman officials. Here he cried out that he was a Pharisee,
knowing that this would cause a fight between the Pharisees and Sadducees. Once again Paul exercised his wisdom
to avoid suffering persecution. As we have seen, Paul faced
his opponents in a different way than Christ did. When
Christ was judged by men for the accomplishment of
redemption, He did not open His mouth (Isa. 53:7; Matt.
26:62-63; 27:12, 14). But Paul, as a faithful and bold apostle
sent by the Lord, exercised his wisdom to save his life from
his persecutors so that he might fulfill the course of his ministry. For the sake of carrying out this ministry, he
endeavored to live as long as possible.

Acts 23:10 goes on to say, "And when much dissension arose, the commander, fearing that Paul might be torn to pieces by them, ordered the soldiers to go down and take him by force from their midst and bring him into the barracks." This was the sovereignty of the Lord to rescue Paul from the hand of the Jews.

ENCOURAGED BY THE LORD

Acts 23:11 says, "But the following night the Lord stood by him and said, Take courage, for as you have solemnly testified concerning Me in Jerusalem, so you must also testify in Rome." The Lord was living all the time in Paul essentially (Gal. 2:20). Now, to strengthen and encourage him, the Lord stood by him economically. This showed the Lord's faithfulness and good care for His servant.

The Lord's word in 23:11 about Paul solemnly testifying concerning Him in Jerusalem indicates that the Lord admitted that the apostle had borne a solemn testimony concerning Him in Jerusalem. Testimony differs from mere teaching. To testify requires experiences of seeing, participation, and enjoyment.

What the ascended Christ wanted to use to carry out His heavenly ministry for the propagating of Himself so that the kingdom of God might be established for the building up of the churches for His fullness was not a group of preachers trained by man's teaching to do a preaching work, but a body of His witnesses, martyrs, who bore a living testimony of the incarnated, crucified, resurrected, and ascended Christ. Witnesses bear a living testimony of the resurrected and ascended Christ in life. They differ from preachers who merely preach doctrines in letters. In His incarnation, Christ carried out His ministry on earth, as recorded in the Gospels, by Himself to sow Himself as the seed of the kingdom of God only in the Jewish land. In His ascension He carries out His ministry in the heavens, as recorded in Acts, through witnesses in His resurrection life and with His ascension power and authority to spread Himself as the development of the kingdom of God from Jerusalem unto the remotest part of the earth, as the consummation of His ministry in the New Testament. All the apostles and disciples in Acts were such witnesses of Christ.

As we shall see, in 26:16 Paul testified that the Lord had appointed him a minister and a witness. A minister is for the ministry; a witness is for the testimony. Ministry is mainly related to work, to what the minister does; testimony is related to the person, to what the witness is.

Satan could instigate the Jewish religionists and utilize the Gentile politicians to bind the apostles and their evangelical ministry, but he could not bind Christ's living witnesses and their living testimonies. The more the Jewish religionists and Gentile politicians bound the apostles and their evangelical ministry, the stronger and brighter these martyrs, these witnesses, of Christ and their living testimonies became. The Lord in 23:11, in His appearing to the apostle, indicated that He would not presently rescue him from his bonds, but that He would leave him in bonds and bring him to Rome so that he might testify concerning Him as he had done in Jerusalem. The Lord encouraged Paul to do this.

In 23:11 the Lord told Paul that he would testify of Him in Rome. This would fulfill Paul's desire, expressed in 19:21, to see Rome. Later, both the Lord's promise and Paul's desire were fulfilled.

Paul was strengthened and encouraged by the Lord's word in verse 11. This word gave Paul the assurance that the Lord would bring him safely from Jerusalem to Rome. Assured by this clear word from the mouth of the Lord, Paul knew that he would go to Rome and there bear the testimony of the Lord Jesus.

THE PLOT OF THE JEWS

Acts 23:12-15 describes the plot of the Jews against Paul. Verses 12 and 13 say, "And when it became day, the Jews formed a plot and put themselves under a curse, saying that they would neither eat nor drink until they had killed Paul. Now there were more than forty who formed this conspiracy."

The plot in verses 12 through 15 manifested the falsehood and satanic hatred (John 8:44; Matt. 23:34) in the hypocritical religionists of Judaism.

In these verses we see how furious the Jews were in hating Paul. The forty who formed the conspiracy may have been young men. They came to the chief priests and elders and said, "We have bound ourselves with a curse to taste nothing until we kill Paul. Now therefore, you inform the commander with the Sanhedrin in order that he may bring him down to you, as though you were intending to determine more accurately the things concerning him; and we, before he draws near, are ready to do away with him" (vv. 14-15). Literally, the Greek words translated, "We have bound ourselves with a curse," mean "We have cursed ourselves with a curse." This is a very strong expression. It seems that the forty conspirators were saying that if they could not kill Paul, then they themselves would not live any longer. It is likely that those who plotted against Paul intended to kill him within twenty-four hours. Their plan was to ambush him as he was brought to the chief priests and elders for further investigation.

SECRETLY TRANSFERRED TO FELIX, THE ROMAN GOVERNOR IN CAESAREA

In 23:16—24:27 we see that Paul was transferred to Felix, the Roman governor in Caesarea. According to 23:16-25, this transfer was carried out secretly. Acts 23:16-18 says, "But the son of Paul's sister heard of the ambush, and he came and entered into the barracks and reported it to Paul. And Paul called one of the centurions to him and said, Bring this young man to the commander, for he has something to report to him. So he took him and brought him to the commander and said, The prisoner Paul called me to him and asked me to bring this young man to you, who has something to tell you." What is recorded here also shows the sovereignty of the Lord to rescue Paul's life.

When the Roman commander heard of the plot against Paul, he exercised his authority and wisdom to send Paul from Jerusalem to Caesarea, where the governor of the province of Judea was. Concerning this, verses 23 and 24 say, "And he called to him a certain two of the centurions and said, Prepare two hundred soldiers that they may go as far as Caesarea, and seventy horsemen, and two hundred spearmen by the third hour of the night, and mounts to stand by to put Paul on that they may bring him safely to Felix the governor." These spearmen may have been slingers, lightly armed soldiers. The third hour of the night was nine o'clock. Felix, to whom Paul was to be brought safely, was the Roman governor of the province of Judea.

The Roman commander exercised his authority to such an extent that he used two hundred soldiers, seventy horsemen, and two hundred spearmen to transfer Paul from Jerusalem to Caesarea. Those who plotted against Paul never imagined that the Roman commander would take such an action. They expected to kill Paul the next day. But during the night, the Roman commander sent Paul out of Jerusalem in the midst of a procession of four hundred seventy soldiers. Here again we see the Lord's sovereignty.

Acts 23:31 says, "So the soldiers, according to what was directed them, took up Paul and brought him by night to Antipatris." Antipatris was a place about forty Roman miles away from Jerusalem and about twenty-six from Caesarea.

Acts 23:33-35 relates what happened once Paul was brought into Caesarea: "And when they had entered into Caesarea and handed over the letter to the governor, they presented also Paul to him. And when he had read it, he asked from what province he was; and learning that he was from Cilicia, he said, I will hear you fully when your accusers also arrive; and he ordered that he be guarded in Herod's praetorium." The praetorium, built by Herod the Great, was the palace of the former kings. It became the official residence of the governor of the Roman province of Judea. Paul was guarded here leniently, not as in the common prison. In the following message we shall see what happened to Paul under Felix, the Roman governor, in Caesarea.

LIFE-STUDY OF ACTS

MESSAGE SIXTY-THREE

THE PROPAGATION
IN ASIA MINOR AND EUROPE
THROUGH THE MINISTRY OF PAUL'S COMPANY

(29)

Scripture Reading: Acts 24:1-27

In this message we come to 24:1-27. In this section of Acts Paul is accused by the Jews' advocate (vv. 1-9), he defends himself before Felix (vv. 10-21), and he is kept in the custody of the unjust and corrupt Roman politician (vv. 22-27).

ACCUSED BY THE JEWS' ADVOCATE

Acts 24:1 says, "And after five days the high priest Ananias came down with some elders and a certain orator, Tertullus; and they informed the governor against Paul." The orator Tertullus, was an advocate, a lawyer, who knew Roman legal procedure.

Verses 2 through 4 continue, "And when he was called, Tertullus began to accuse him saying, Since we have obtained much peace through you, and through your forethought reforms are being carried out for this nation, both in every way and everywhere we welcome it, most excellent Felix, with all thankfulness. But that I may not detain you further, I entreat you to hear us briefly in your forbearance." Tertullus' word here displayed his baseness; he was altogether without any ethical standard.

In 24:5 Tertullus said concerning Paul, "For we have found this man a pest and an agitator of insurrections among all the Jews throughout the inhabited earth, and a ringleader of the sect of the Nazarenes." Here we have a threefold accusation. First, Tertullus accused Paul of being

a pest. A pest is full of evil "germs." Paul, however, was full of
positive germs—the germs of the resurrected Christ for the
propagation of Christ by imparting Him to others. We all
should be such "pests."

Second, Tertullus gave to Paul the title of "agitator." He
accused Paul of being an agitator of insurrections among the
Jews throughout the inhabited earth.

Third, Tertullus claimed that Paul was a ringleader of
the sect of the Nazarenes. The word "sect" here is somewhat
equal to today's word "cult." Tertullus' word indicates that
the Jews regarded the believers in the Lord Jesus as Nazarenes. In chapter thirteen of Acts the believers were first
called Christians in Antioch. Christians are Christ-men,
those who live Christ. Here the Jews' attorney gives the
believers another nickname—Nazarenes. The use of this
nickname indicates that the believers were considered followers of the Nazarene, Jesus.

DEFENDING HIMSELF BEFORE FELIX

In 24:10 Paul begins to make his defense before Felix:
"And when the governor had nodded for him to speak, Paul
answered, Knowing that for many years you have been a
judge to this nation, I cheerfully make my defense as to the
things concerning myself." We have seen that, in contrast to
the way the Lord Jesus faced His opponents, it was necessary for Paul to make a defense and to exercise his wisdom
in order to save his life from his persecutors so that he might
fulfill the course of his ministry.

Serving God and
Behaving according to the Scriptures

In verses 11 through 14 Paul goes on to say, "As you can
realize, it is not more than twelve days since I went up to
worship in Jerusalem. And neither in the temple did they
find me disputing with anyone nor stirring up a crowd,
neither in the synagogues nor throughout the city. Neither
are they able to prove to you the things concerning which
they now accuse me. But I confess this to you, that according

to the way which they call a sect, so I serve the God of our fathers, believing all that is written throughout the Law and in the Prophets." Here we see that what the opposing Jews called a sect Paul called the way. As we have pointed out, the way, mentioned several times in Acts (9:2; 18:25-26; 19:9, 23; 22:4), denotes the Lord's full salvation in God's New Testament economy.

In verse 14 Paul testified that according to the way the opposers called a sect he served the God of their fathers. Literally, the Greek word rendered "serve" means "serve as a priest." Paul's way of serving God was the way of the New Testament economy. Therefore, his way of serving was different from that of the other Jews.

In verse 14 Paul also says that he believed all that is written throughout the Law and in the Prophets. Here Paul is saying that he acted according to the Old Testament, which was composed of the Law and the Prophets. Therefore, Paul vindicated himself as a person who behaved according to the Scriptures.

A Resurrection
of the Righteous and the Unrighteous

In 24:15 Paul speaks of the resurrection: "Having hope toward God, which these themselves also look for, that there is about to be a resurrection both of the righteous and the unrighteous." The resurrection of the righteous will occur before the millennium at the Lord's coming back (1 Cor. 15:23; 1 Thes. 4:16). It will be the resurrection of life (John 5:28-29a; Dan. 12:2). The resurrection of life is the resurrection of the saved believers before the millennium. The dead believers will be resurrected to enjoy eternal life at the coming back of the Lord Jesus. Hence, it is called the resurrection of life. It is also the resurrection of reward (Luke 14:14), when God will reward the saints (Rev. 11:18) at the Lord's return (1 Cor. 4:5).

The resurrection of the righteous, which is the resurrection of life, also includes the first, or the best, resurrection (Rev. 20:4-6). Revelation 20:5 and 6 speak of the first, or the best, resurrection. The first resurrection is the best one. It is not only the resurrection of life, but also the resurrection of reward, the ex-resurrection, that is, the extraordinary resurrection for which the apostle Paul sought (Phil. 3:11), the resurrection of kingship as a reward to the overcomers so that they may reign as co-kings with Christ in the millennial kingdom (Rev. 20:4, 6). Not only the resurrected overcomers, such as the man-child in Revelation 12:5 and the later martyrs in Revelation 15:2, but also the raptured living ones, such as the firstfruit in Revelation 14:1-5, will have "part in the first resurrection" (Rev. 20:6).

In Philippians 3:11 Paul refers to the first, or best, resurrection as the out-resurrection: "If by any means I may attain to the out-resurrection from among the dead." This is the outstanding resurrection, the extra-resurrection, which will be a prize to the overcoming saints. All believers who are dead in Christ will participate in the resurrection from among the dead at the Lord's coming back (1 Thes. 4:16; 1 Cor. 15:52). But the overcoming saints will enjoy an extra, outstanding portion of that resurrection. This is called in Hebrews 11:35 the "better resurrection."

To arrive at the out-resurrection means that our entire being has been gradually and continually resurrected. God first resurrected our deadened spirit (John 5:25; Eph. 2:5-6). Then from our spirit He proceeds to resurrect our soul (Rom. 8:6) and our mortal body (Rom. 8:11), until our entire being—spirit, soul, and body—is fully resurrected out of our old being by and with His life. This is a process in life through which we must pass and a race for us to run until we arrive at the out-resurrection as the prize. Hence, the out-resurrection should be the goal and destination of our Christian life. We can reach this goal only by being conformed to the death of Christ (Phil. 3:10), by living a crucified life. In the death of Christ we are processed in resurrection from the old creation to the new.

We have pointed out that in Acts 24:15 Paul says that there will be a resurrection both of the righteous and the unrighteous. The resurrection of the unrighteous will occur after the millennium (Rev. 20:5). It will be the resurrection of judgment (John 5:29) and of shame and everlasting contempt (Dan. 12:2b). This resurrection of judgment will be the resurrection of the perished unbelievers after the millennium (Rev. 20:5, 12). All the dead unbelievers will be resurrected after the thousand years to be judged at the great white throne (Rev. 20:11-15). Hence, it is called the resurrection of judgment. In Revelation 20:12 the word "standing" indicates the dead have been resurrected. This is the resurrection of judgment for eternal perdition upon the unrighteous after the millennium. This is the resurrection concerning which the apostle Paul warned unrighteous Felix in Acts 24:25.

All the unsaved will be in the resurrection of judgment. Because they will be condemned to eternal perdition, their resurrection will be of shame and everlasting contempt. Paul, in his wisdom, mentioned this resurrection as a warning to Felix. Paul's word implies that Felix should prepare himself to face the coming resurrection of judgment. As we shall see, later on Paul spoke directly to Felix concerning the coming judgment.

Paul's Exercise to Have a Conscience without Offense

In 24:16 Paul said to Felix, "In this I also exercise myself, to have always a conscience without offense toward God and men." Paul uttered a similar word when he defended himself before the Sanhedrin: "I have conducted myself in all good conscience before God until this day" (23:1). We have seen that for Paul to conduct himself in all good conscience before God was a great return to God from man's fall. Paul spoke such a word to vindicate himself before those who accused him of being a lawless and even a reckless person. Paul's testimony in 23:1 and 24:16 concerning his conscience showed his high standard of morality in contrast to the hypocrisy of the Jewish religionists and the crookedness of the Roman politicians. As we continue on in Acts 24, we shall see more concerning the corruption of Roman politics.

KEPT IN THE CUSTODY OF THE UNJUST
AND CORRUPT ROMAN POLITICIAN

Acts 24:22 and 23 say, "But Felix, knowing more accurately the things concerning the way, adjourned the case, saying, When Lysias the commander comes down, I will determine your affairs. And he directed the centurion to keep him in custody, and yet that he should have some liberty, and that no one should prevent his own people from attending to him." Literally, the Greek word rendered "the case" in verse 22 means "them." The Greek word for "liberty" in verse 23 also means relief, ease.

According to verse 24, "After some days, Felix arrived with Drusilla his wife, who was a Jewess, and he sent for Paul and heard him concerning his faith in Christ Jesus." Drusilla was a daughter of King Herod Agrippa. She was persuaded by Felix, who became enamored of her, to forsake her husband and marry him. This showed the intemperance and corruption of Felix, a Roman politician. He was an immoral person without self-control.

Verse 24 says that Felix heard Paul concerning his faith in Christ Jesus. Literally, the Greek word translated "his" means "the."

Reasoning concerning Righteousness,
Self-control, and the Coming Judgment

Acts 24:25 says, "And as he was reasoning concerning righteousness, and self-control, and the coming judgment, Felix became afraid and answered, Go for the present, and when I have an opportunity, I will call for you." Literally, the Greek word rendered "was reasoning" means to say thoroughly, discuss (in argument or exhortation), dispute; the same as in 17:2 and 18:4, 19.

Realizing Felix's unrighteousness (vv. 26-27) and intemperance, the apostle reasoned with him of righteousness and self-control, the control of passions and desires, especially here regarding the controlling of sexual desires. The coming judgment is related to the resurrection of the unrighteous, which the apostle preached in verse 15. The apostle also reasoned with Felix of the coming judgment as a warning. Through this Felix became afraid.

Felix certainly was an unrighteous politician. As verse 26 indicates, he hoped to receive money from Paul. He expected a bribe, the giving of money unrighteously. Based upon this fact, Paul reasoned with him concerning righteousness.

We have seen that Felix also lacked self-control. Because of Felix's intemperate lust, Paul, in order to show Felix's sinfulness, also reasoned with him concerning self-control.

Eventually, in his reasoning with Felix, Paul came to the matter of the future judgment for perdition. In their preaching to the Gentiles, both Peter in 10:42 and Paul here and in 17:31 stressed the coming judgment of God. The resurrected Christ at His coming back will be the Judge of the living before the millennium on His throne of glory (Matt. 25:31-46). This is related to His second coming (2 Tim. 4:1). He will also be the Judge of the dead after the millennium on the great white throne (Rev. 20:11-15).

Paul's word to Felix was a strong warning. Felix became afraid, but he was not moved. Sending Paul away, he said, "Go for the present, and when I have an opportunity, I will call for you" (v. 25).

Felix did send for Paul a number of times. Concerning this, 24:26 says, "At the same time also he was hoping that money would be given him by Paul; wherefore also he sent for him more frequently and conversed with him." This indicates the Roman politician's corruption. His intention in sending for Paul was not to hear the gospel; rather, his purpose was to get money.

Two Years in Caesarea

Verse 27 concludes, "And when two years were completed, Felix was succeeded by Porcius Festus; and wanting to gain favor with the Jews, Felix left Paul bound." Porcius Festus was the successor of Felix as the governor of Judea. Felix's leaving Paul bound again shows the corruption of Roman politics.

Luke does not disclose what the apostle did during these two years in Caesarea. Paul may have used the time to be with the Lord for His move on earth. If so, this may have influenced the Epistles he wrote during the time of his appeal in Rome—Colossians, Ephesians, and Philippians—which are the most mysterious, most profound, and the richest in the divine revelation.

A PICTURE OF HYPOCRISY AND CORRUPTION

In these chapters of Acts we have a picture of hypocrisy in religion and corruption in politics. What hypocrisy there was in Judaism! The Jews pretended to serve God, to please God, and to glorify God, yet they did many evil things. These chapters expose the evil of the Jewish people. They were religious in an evil way, even plotting to kill Paul. Although they were evil, they still pretended to be those who worshipped God and pleased Him. Hence, in Judaism there was hypocrisy.

In Roman politics we see corruption and unrighteousness. Felix knew that Paul had not done anything wrong. Therefore, in justice Felix should have released Paul. However, in order to gain favor with the Jews and with the hope of receiving money from Paul and his friends, he kept Paul in custody for two years. Felix allowed Paul's friends to visit him, but his purpose in doing so was to receive money. As a result, in an unrighteous way Paul was kept in custody for two years. In the following message we shall consider what Paul might have done during those years.

LIFE-STUDY OF ACTS

MESSAGE SIXTY-FOUR

THE PROPAGATION
IN ASIA MINOR AND EUROPE
THROUGH THE MINISTRY OF PAUL'S COMPANY

(30)

Scripture Reading: Acts 24:22-27; Gal. 1:17; Col. 1:25; 1 Tim. 1:3-4; 2 Tim. 1:14; 2:2, 22

In 24:1-9 Paul was accused by the Jews' advocate, and in 24:10-21 he defended himself before Felix, the Roman governor of Judea. Then in 24:22-27 he was kept in the custody of the unjust and corrupt Roman politician. Acts 24:27 says, "And when two years were completed, Felix was succeeded by Porcius Festus; and wanting to gain favor with the Jews, Felix left Paul bound." Luke does not disclose what Paul did during these two years. In this message we shall consider what Paul might have done during this period of time.

RECEIVING REVELATION
THROUGH THE KNOWLEDGE OF THE OLD TESTAMENT

Luke does not tell us anything about the two years Paul was kept in custody in Caesarea. Neither does Luke say anything about the time Paul spent in Arabia after his conversion. Concerning this, Paul says, "Neither did I go up to Jerusalem to those who were apostles before me, but I went away to Arabia, and again returned to Damascus" (Gal. 1:17). It is difficult to trace where in Arabia Paul went and how long he stayed there after his conversion. However, it must have been a place apart from the Christians, and the time of his stay there must not have been short. His purpose in referring to this was to testify that he did not receive the gospel from man (Gal. 1:12). In Arabia Paul must have received some revelation concerning the gospel directly from the Lord.

No doubt, the divine revelation Paul received from the Lord in Arabia came through his knowledge of the Old Testament. Paul was an excellent student of the Old Testament. This is indicated by the way he expounded the Old Testament in the books of Romans, Galatians, and Hebrews. As we read these books, we see that Paul had a thorough knowledge of the Old Testament. Furthermore, he had insight into the Scriptures. An example of this insight is Paul's allegorizing Sarah, Abraham's wife, and Hagar, Abraham's concubine, as two covenants (Gal. 4:22-26). Apart from Paul's allegorizing of these women in Galatians 4, we could read Genesis again and again without seeing that Sarah and Hagar signify two covenants. But Paul, who was very knowledgeable in the truth in the Old Testament, had the insight to see this. Through his knowledge of the Old Testament the divine light came to him. Therefore, as indicated by his writings, Paul could understand the types in the Old Testament concerning Christ's Person and work. Paul's knowledge of the Scriptures was one reason for his receiving so much divine revelation.

RECEIVING REVELATION DIRECTLY FROM THE LORD

Although Paul received a great deal of revelation from the Lord through his knowledge of the Old Testament, certain aspects of the revelation he received from the Lord are not based on the Old Testament. We may take as an example what Paul says concerning the different kinds of law in Romans 7 and 8. In Romans 8:2 he says, "For the law of the Spirit of life in Christ Jesus has freed me from the law of sin and of death." Here Paul speaks of two laws—the law of sin and death and the law of the Spirit of life. In Romans 7, in addition to the law of God (v. 22), Paul speaks of "the law of my mind" (v. 23), which is the law of doing good. In Romans 7:23 he also mentions "the law of sin which is in my members." Therefore, in these two chapters Paul speaks of four laws: the written law of God, the law of doing good, the law of sin and death, and the law of the Spirit of life. In contrast to the law of God, the law of doing good, the law of sin and death, and the law of the Spirit of life are not written laws. Rather, they are fixed principles of life.

Every kind of life has its own law. The law of doing good is the law of the human life. The law of sin and death is the law of the sinful, Satanic life. The law of the Spirit of life is the law of the divine life. These three laws are based on the fixed principles of these kinds of life. The human life has its own law, the satanic life has a sinful law, and the divine life, which is the highest life, surely has a divine law.

What was the source of the revelation Paul saw concerning these three laws? I have investigated this matter in the attempt to learn the source, but I have not been able to find it. Probably Paul received the revelation concerning these three laws directly from the Lord. Moreover, his knowledge of these laws was based on his experience. Paul experienced the law of the mind, the law of doing good. Paul also experienced the law of sin and death. Concerning this, he could say, "I see a different law in my members, warring against the law of my mind and making me a captive in the law of sin which is in my members" (Rom. 7:23). Earlier in Romans 7 Paul said, "For I know that in me, that is, in my flesh, nothing good dwells; for to will is present with me, but to do the good is not. For the good which I will, I do not; but the evil I do not will, this I practice. But if what I do not will, this I do, it is no longer I that do it but sin that dwells in me. I find then the law that, at my willing to do the good, the evil is present with me" (vv. 18-21). Therefore, from his experience Paul learned that there is such a law as the law of sin and death. To be sure, from his Christian experience Paul discovered that there is a higher law within him—the law of the divine life. Paul certainly received the revelation concerning the law of doing good, the law of sin and death, and the law of the Spirit of life.

Because Paul received so much revelation from the Lord, when he came forth to preach, he could minister to others the riches of these revelations. He was able to write such letters as 1 and 2 Thessalonians, Romans, Galatians, and 1 and 2 Corinthians. As we read Paul's writings, we see that each one of them is full of divine revelation. The point we are emphasizing here is that Paul must have received a great deal of revelation from the Lord during the time he was in Arabia.

PAUL IN CAESAREA

According to Acts 24:27, the Lord set aside a two-year period in which Paul was kept in custody in Caesarea. In these years Paul must have thought about what had taken place in Acts 15 and 21.

In Acts 21 we see the weakness of Paul in facing the religious mixture in Jerusalem. Although Peter and John were with the Lord on the Mount of Transfiguration, they were silent concerning God's New Testament economy in Acts 21. As we have seen, James spoke on behalf of the believing Jews who were still zealous for the law (21:20). Did James not have any light concerning God's New Testament economy? It seems that he was very dull in his understanding of this. Although Peter and John had been enlightened regarding God's New Testament economy, they did not do anything about the situation of the mixture of the New Testament grace with the Old Testament law in Jerusalem. It seems that Paul was the only one burdened about that situation.

As we consider the scene portrayed in these chapters of Acts, we see that the central figure was actually the Lord Himself. He played the major role in these chapters as the One who was sovereign over everything. Eventually, the Lord delivered Paul from the difficult situation in Jerusalem, preserving his life from the plotting Jews, and placed him in custody under the Roman government in Caesarea. Although Paul was in custody, he was not actually in prison. Felix "directed the centurion to keep him in custody, and yet that he should have some liberty, and that no one should prevent his own people from attending to him" (24:23). As 24:26 indicates, Felix's purpose in allowing Paul's friends to visit him was to gain money for himself. Although Felix's purpose was to get money, the Lord had His own purpose in keeping Paul in custody in Caesarea. There in Caesarea Paul did not have anything to do, and he was safely kept from trouble.

PREPARED TO WRITE MORE EPISTLES

What do you think Paul did during those two years of custody in Caesarea? Do you think that, after having passed through so much turmoil, Paul did nothing except read the Scriptures? Paul surely must have recalled his experiences in chapters fifteen and twenty-one. He must have thought about the things through which he had passed. He might have compared his recent experiences with the revelation he had received in the past, especially with the revelation he had received in Arabia. I believe that Paul reviewed the entire situation from Acts 15 onward in the light of the revelation that had been given to him. As he reviewed matters in this way, the light may have become clearer and clearer. This, of course, is our inference based upon the study of the New Testament.

As Paul considered the situation in Acts 21, he may have felt unhappy with James and also with Peter and John. He may have regretted what had happened. Then Paul may have realized that it was necessary for him to write more Epistles. The content of Hebrews, Ephesians, Philippians, and Colossians may have been deep within him during the years in Caesarea.

I have spent time studying what Paul did for two years in Caesarea. I believe that during this time Paul reviewed his experience from Acts 15 and 21, comparing it with the revelation he had received from the Lord and with the situation he had observed in Jerusalem with James, Peter, and John. I believe that the more Paul reviewed his experience, the more burdened he became to put out further writings. Paul may have realized that he would not soon be released from the custody of the Roman government. He may have anticipated a lengthy stay in Caesarea. I believe that during the two years he was there, he was prepared by the

Lord to write the eight Epistles of Hebrews, Ephesians, Philippians, Colossians, 1 and 2 Timothy, Titus, and Philemon.

Books like Hebrews and Ephesians could not have been written without adequate preparation. The writing of such Epistles requires a great deal of preparation. Before Paul could write Hebrews and Ephesians, he first had to enter into the depths of God's revelation. Before writing these Epistles, he needed a time of thorough consideration. Paul was given this time, a time of preparation, during the two years he was kept in custody in Caesarea. Later, when he was transferred from Caesarea to Rome, he had the opportunity to put out the books of Hebrews, Ephesians, Philippians, and Colossians. Of course, he was also able to write 1 and 2 Timothy, Titus, and Philemon. It would be very helpful to review especially Hebrews, Ephesians, Philippians, and Colossians against the background of Acts 15 through 24. If we do this, we shall visualize these four Epistles in a new way with more light.

BURDENED CONCERNING
GOD'S NEW TESTAMENT ECONOMY

Paul was heavily burdened concerning God's New Testament economy. Although he was not able to continue to work this out personally, he was given the opportunity to write the divine revelation. In Colossians 1:25 he says, "I became a minister according to the stewardship of God, which was given to me for you, to complete the word of God." Here we see that Paul's writing of the book of Colossians was for the completing of God's New Testament economy. Without the books of Colossians, Philippians, Ephesians, and Hebrews, we would not have a clear view of God's New Testament economy.

Actually, the Greek word for "economy" (*oikonomia*) is a word used particularly by Paul, especially in the book of Ephesians. Although Paul uses this word in 1 Corinthians 9:17, he does not use it there for the specific purpose of unveiling God's New Testament economy. But he does use the word *oikonomia* for this purpose in Ephesians. Ephesians, we know, is a book on the church. But if we have only this understanding of Ephesians, our comprehension of this book will be too superficial. We need to see that Ephesians is a book on God's economy.

We have emphasized the fact that regarding the situation in Acts we can see the Lord's sovereignty. Neither Judaism nor Roman politics could defeat the sovereign Lord. On the contrary, everything served His purpose. Even Peter's fearfulness (Gal. 2:12) and the plots of the Jews served the Lord's purpose. Apparently, these things frustrated His move. Actually, they served His purpose in revealing and then carrying out God's New Testament economy.

Today we are burdened for the carrying out of God's New Testament economy. This is the reason I have often pointed out that in the Lord's recovery we are not doing an ordinary Christian work. On the contrary, by the Lord's mercy and grace, we are here to carry out God's New Testament economy.

SEEING THE VISION
OF GOD'S NEW TESTAMENT ECONOMY

After studying all the books of the Bible for many years, we began to see the overall revelation in the Scriptures concerning God's New Testament economy. Through the Word, the Lord showed us that in this economy the Triune God became a man in the Son. This means that the accomplishment of God's New Testament economy began with the incarnation. Through Christ's human living, death, resurrection, and ascension, everything necessary for the accomplishment of God's economy was done. After breathing the Spirit into the disciples essentially (John 20:22), the Lord, in His ascension, poured out the Spirit upon His Body economically (Acts 2:17). That outpouring of the Spirit was the completion of the accomplishment of God's New Testament economy. Now the Triune God as the processed all-inclusive Spirit is both within His chosen people and upon them, and with them He is carrying out the New Testament economy. The Lord is propagating Himself by imparting Himself to His believers to make them living members of His universal Body to be His corporate vessel for His expression. Today this corporate vessel is expressed in various localities as local churches, and all these churches are lampstands shining in this dark age. Eventually, all the shining local churches will consummate in the New Jerusalem, which will be the ultimate consummation of God's move in His New Testament economy.

The crucial focus of God's New Testament economy is the all-inclusive Christ as our life, our person, and our everything. The divine economy is not focused on any law, regulation, teaching, philosophy, or practice. God's economy is focused on one all-inclusive, wonderful Person. This Person is the embodiment of the processed Triune God, and He is realized as the all-inclusive life-giving Spirit, who is within us and upon us. This Spirit is working in us so that we may be brought back directly to Christ to enjoy Him as everything. I hope that we shall all have a clear view concerning this.

If we see the vision of the divine economy, we shall praise the Lord for the two years He kept Paul in custody in Caesarea. Those years were a time of preparation for Paul, a chosen vessel, to put forth the completing revelation which he received of the Lord. After the preparation in Caesarea, Paul was transferred to Rome. Then he wrote the excellent completing Epistles of Ephesians, Philippians, Colossians, and Hebrews. If we would be constituted of Paul's ministry, we need to study these four books.

In addition to writing these four Epistles, Paul also wrote 1 and 2 Timothy, Titus, and Philemon. In 1 Timothy 1:3 and 4 Paul said to Timothy, "Even as I urged you, when I was going into Macedonia, to remain in Ephesus in order that you might charge certain ones not to teach differently, nor to occupy themselves with myths and unending genealogies, which give occasion for questionings rather than God's dispensation which is in faith." Here Paul charged us not to teach differently, but to teach God's economy. According to the Epistle of 1 Timothy, God's economy is focused on God manifested in the flesh (1 Tim. 3:16). According to 1 Timothy 3:15, the church of the living God, the house of God, is the pillar and base of the truth, and this truth is actually the reality of the New Testament economy.

In 2 Timothy 1:14 we have this charge: "Guard the good deposit through the Holy Spirit who dwells in us." Then in 2 Timothy 2:2 Paul went on to say, "The things which you have heard from me through many witnesses, these commit to faithful men, who will be competent to teach others also." Here Paul charged Timothy to pass on to others what he had received so that they might in turn teach others.

Furthermore, Paul told Timothy to "pursue righteousness, faith, love, peace with those who call on the Lord out of a pure heart" (2 Tim. 2:22). Here we see that calling on the name of the Lord has a definite place in the carrying out of the New Testament economy of God. For the carrying out of God's New Testament economy, we need to call on the name of the Lord continually. Not only should we ourselves call individually; we should also call on Him with those who call on the Lord out of a pure heart.

We thank the Lord for the last eight Epistles written by Paul. If we did not have these books, I do not know where we would be today with respect to God's New Testament economy. We also thank the Lord for the picture portrayed for us in Acts. After considering the remaining chapters of this book, we shall have an even clearer view of the carrying out of God's New Testament economy.

LIFE-STUDY OF ACTS

MESSAGE SIXTY-FIVE

THE PROPAGATION
IN ASIA MINOR AND EUROPE
THROUGH THE MINISTRY OF PAUL'S COMPANY

(31)

Scripture Reading: Acts 25:1-27

In the last four chapters of Acts, chapters twenty-five through twenty-eight, Paul defends himself twice. First, he defends himself before Festus (25:6-8), and then before Agrippa (26:1-29). Following his defense before Agrippa, Paul makes his fourth journey (27:1—28:31). In these chapters we have a picture of people in three kinds of situations. We have a picture of the Jewish religionists, the Roman politicians, and those in the church.

THE JEWISH RELIGIONISTS

Let us first consider the portrait of the Jewish religionists. Judaism was formed according to God's word. Therefore, the Jewish religion was according to the Scriptures. The Jewish religionists had the holy Bible, the holy land, the holy city, the holy temple, the holy priesthood, and all the other holy things. Nevertheless, what these religious people did as recorded in the book of Acts was absolutely not of God but of Satan.

Acts 25:1-3 says, "Festus therefore, having come into the province, after three days went up to Jerusalem from Caesarea. And the chief priests and leading men of the Jews informed him against Paul; and they kept entreating him, asking for a favor against him, so that he might summon him to Jerusalem, setting an ambush to do away with him on the way." Here we see that the Jews wanted to set up an ambush in order to kill Paul. Furthermore, the Jewish religionists lied and exercised hypocrisy. With them there was nothing holy or righteous. With them there was nothing that could be counted as being for God. In this religion we cannot see anything spiritual or divine. On the contrary, what was practiced among the Jewish religionists in the case of Paul was not only fleshly and sinful but even devilish and hellish. The source of what they did was the Devil.

THE ROMAN POLITICIANS

In Acts we also have a portrait of the Roman politicians. In particular, we have an account concerning the commander, Felix, Festus, and Agrippa. The higher the Roman politicians were, the more corrupt they were. Felix was more corrupt than the commander, Festus was more corrupt than Felix, and Agrippa was more corrupt than Festus. According to the record in the holy Word, in the Roman political circle there was much corruption. As we have pointed out, along with the Hebrew religion and Greek culture, Roman politics was one of the three elements that composed western culture. But according to Acts, Roman politics was corrupt.

Acts 24:24 speaks of Felix and Drusilla his wife. Drusilla was a daughter of King Herod Agrippa. Felix became enamored of her and persuaded her to forsake her husband and marry him. This shows the intemperance and corruption of Felix, a Roman politician. Felix's corruption is also seen in his sending for Paul frequently in the hope that money would be given him by Paul (24:26).

Acts 25:13 speaks of Agrippa and Bernice. Bernice was a sister of Drusilla, the wife of Felix. She was also a sister of Agrippa, with whom she lived incestuously. This may be the reason that in 25:13 Bernice is not identified as being Agrippa's wife. Roman politics certainly was dark and corrupt, full of sexual immorality and the love of money. The record in Acts exposes the corruption of the Roman politicians.

THE DISAPPOINTING SITUATION
CONCERNING THE CHURCH IN JERUSALEM

In 1 Corinthians 10:32 Paul speaks of the Jews, the Greeks, and the church of God. This indicates that in New Testament times people were of three classes: the Jews— God's chosen people; the Greeks—unbelieving Gentiles; and the church—a composition of the believers in Christ. We have seen that, according to the picture portrayed in Acts, the Jewish religionists were hypocritical and even devilish and that the Roman politicians were dark and corrupt. What, then, was the situation concerning the church? When Paul was in custody for two years in Caesarea, he must have been disappointed with the church in Jerusalem. What he saw in the church there was weakness and compromise.

Paul, as a vessel chosen by God, was enlightened to the uttermost concerning the universe. In 2 Corinthians, an Epistle written not long before his last trip to Jerusalem, Paul testifies that he was caught away to the third heaven (2 Cor. 12:2) and was also caught away into paradise (v. 4), the pleasant section in Hades. Having received an abundance of revelation, Paul was enlightened concerning the secrets of the universe. Of course, he received much revelation in particular concerning God's New Testament economy. Now, in the last chapters of Acts, Paul was in a situation in which he was surrounded by the Jewish religionists, the Roman politicians, and his fellow workers in the church life. He must have found this situation very disappointing.

Weakness, Compromise,
and the Lack of Revelation

As one who had an abundance of the divine revelation stored up in his being, Paul faced the situation among the Jews, the Roman politicians, and the church people. Among the Jewish religionists he saw hypocrisy, and among the Roman politicians he saw corruption. Furthermore, in the church life he saw weakness, compromise, and the lack of light and revelation. It seems that no one in the church was bold enough to stand for the revelation they had received and the vision they had seen. In the midst of that situation Peter should have stood boldly for the revelation he had received of the Lord, but he failed to do this.

In chapters two through five of Acts Peter and John were very strong and bold. As a result of their boldness, they were brought before the Sanhedrin in chapter four, and they were placed by the Sanhedrin in public custody in chapter five. There was no sign of weakness or compromise in Peter and John in these early chapters. There is no hint that they were afraid of the Jewish religionists or compromised with them. However, as we read from Acts 15 onward and also read Galatians 2, we see that Peter eventually was exposed in his weakness and even in his hypocrisy.

The Destruction of Jerusalem

Because of the strong attitude and standing taken by Peter, John, and the other believers, the Jews persecuted the saints to such an extent that, with the exception of the apostles, they all left Jerusalem (8:1). But by the time Paul paid his last visit to Jerusalem in Acts 21, James could speak of "how many thousands there are among the Jews who have believed, and all are zealous for the law" (v. 20). All these thousands of believers had remained in Jerusalem. If Peter and John had had the strong attitude and standing in chapter twenty-one that they had in chapters two through five, most of these Jewish believers would have been scattered, and that scattering would have become their salvation as far as the religious mixture in Jerusalem was concerned. However, these thousands of believers, who were still zealous for the law, stayed in Jerusalem, and their remaining in Jerusalem put them in great danger. Not too long after Paul's last visit to Jerusalem, perhaps not more than ten years later, Titus came with the Roman army to destroy Jerusalem and to slaughter those who continued to live there. It is possible that many Christians were put to death at that time.

In the parables in Matthew 21:33-46 and 22:1-14 the Lord Jesus expressed God's anger concerning the situation in Jerusalem. The Lord indicated that God, "the lord of the vineyard," would miserably destroy the evil vinedressers. This was fulfilled when Titus, the Roman prince, and his army destroyed Jerusalem in A.D. 70. In Matthew 22:7 the Lord prophesied that God would send "his troops," the Roman troops under Titus, and destroy the city of Jerusalem. The destruction of Jerusalem may have included the church in Jerusalem. Because of James' compromising attitude and Peter's weakness, the church in Jerusalem may have been destroyed along with the city. However, the situation concerning the church would have been different if Peter and John had been as bold in Acts 21 as they were at the beginning. If they had continued to be strong and bold, the saints either would have been scattered, or would have been persecuted unto death by the Jewish religionists.

The Martyrdom of James

According to history, the James of Acts 21 was martyred at the hands of the opposing Jews. The leaders of the Sanhedrin thought that James was very favorable toward Judaism. They called together a congregation and asked James to speak to them, thinking that he would speak positively about Judaism. James, however, was faithful to preach Christ in a strong way. The leaders of the Sanhedrin were offended, and they put James to death. They had received a mistaken impression of James because so many Jewish believers in Jerusalem were zealous for the law. This may have caused the leaders of the Sanhedrin to think that James was for Judaism.

From the record in Acts 21 we see that James even went so far as to push Paul into the "trap" of an extremely difficult situation. As we have pointed out, the Lord did not tolerate that compromising situation in Jerusalem.

PAUL'S LAST JOURNEY TO JERUSALEM

It is difficult to believe that Peter and John were silent about the situation in Jerusalem. They should have borne the burden to clear up the matter. It should not have been necessary for Paul to do this. But Peter and James did not do their duty in Jerusalem. Rather, the church there was allowed to remain in a declining condition, and Paul should have been very unhappy about that situation. Although he was heavily burdened to carry out God's New Testament economy in the Gentile world, he realized that the source in Jerusalem had been contaminated and that the flow of the poison was spreading into the Gentile world. As Paul's Epistles indicate, he had to face the Judaizers everywhere. According to the book of Galatians, the churches in Galatia were troubled by the Judaizers. Therefore, Paul knew that he could not continue his work in the Gentile world until the situation in Jerusalem had been dealt with. Knowing that the main thing that was damaging the church life in the Gentile world was Judaism, Paul was burdened to go back to Jerusalem. This was the reason he purposed in his spirit to go to Jerusalem (19:21). He was burdened to deal with the source of the contamination.

In reading chapters eighteen through twenty-one of Acts, it is difficult for us to decide whether or not Paul was right in going to Jerusalem the last time. Acts 19:21 says, "And when these things were fulfilled, Paul purposed in his spirit, having passed through Macedonia and Achaia, to go to Jerusalem, saying, After I have been there, I must also see Rome." In 20:22 and 23 Paul said, "And now, behold, I am going bound in the spirit to Jerusalem, not knowing what I will meet with there, except that the Holy Spirit solemnly testifies to me in city after city, saying that bonds and afflictions await me." The Holy Spirit's testimony was a prophecy, a foretelling, not a charge. When Paul was in Tyre, the disciples "told Paul through the Spirit not to set foot in Jerusalem" (21:4). Here, having made known to Paul that bonds and afflictions awaited him in Jerusalem, the Spirit took a further step to tell him through some members of the Body not to go to Jerusalem. Furthermore, the prophet Agabus "took Paul's girdle; and having bound his own feet and hands, he said, Thus says the Holy Spirit, In this way shall the Jews in Jerusalem bind the man whose girdle this is and deliver him into the hands of the Gentiles"

(21:11). Luke goes on to say, "And when we heard these things, both we and those in that place entreated him not to go up to Jerusalem. Then Paul answered, What are you doing, weeping and breaking my heart? For I am ready not only to be bound, but also to die in Jerusalem for the name of the Lord Jesus. And when he would not be persuaded, we were silent, having said, The will of the Lord be done" (vv. 12-14). The more we consider all these verses, the more we realize how difficult it is to decide whether Paul was right or wrong in going up to Jerusalem the last time. On the one hand, the Spirit indicated to Paul that bonds and afflictions awaited him in Jerusalem. On the other hand, through members of the Body, the Spirit told Paul not to go to Jerusalem. The Lord was very clear about the situation there.

ENCOURAGED BY THE LORD

By the Lord's sovereignty Paul was rescued from the hand of the rioting Jews into the hand of the Roman commander (21:27-39). After Paul defended himself before the Jews (21:40—22:21), was bound by the Romans (22:22-29), and defended himself before the Sanhedrin (22:30—23:10), he was encouraged by the Lord. Concerning this, 23:11 says, "But the following night the Lord stood by him and said, Take courage, for as you have solemnly testified concerning Me in Jerusalem, so you must also testify in Rome." This was a word of strong assurance to Paul. Surely Paul was afraid. If he had not been afraid, there would have been no need for the Lord to tell him to take courage. Paul certainly had been in a very frightening situation. But sovereignly the Lord rescued him from that situation, and then He came to assure him that he would testify of Him in Rome. In this way Paul's desire to see Rome would be fulfilled.

PAUL'S VISION OF GOD'S NEW TESTAMENT ECONOMY

Let us consider again the picture of the situation in which Paul found himself. The church was weak, compromising, and lacking in light. With the church in Jerusalem there was not a genuine testimony. The religious people in

Judaism were blind, devilish, and full of hatred, and the Roman politicians were corrupt. Against such a background we see Paul, a man burdened for and saturated with God's New Testament economy. As Paul considered the situation involving the church, Judaism, and the Roman government, he knew that what was needed most was God's New Testament economy.

What is God's New Testament economy? God's New Testament economy is to propagate the processed Triune God in the Person of the all-inclusive, resurrected Christ. Only the propagation of this resurrected Christ is the answer to the pitiful situation on the earth. What is needed is for us to allow God to carry out His New Testament economy in propagating the resurrected Christ. Paul must have considered this very much during the two years custody in Caesarea. Therefore, when he was brought to Rome, he began to write the last eight of his Epistles: Colossians, Ephesians, Philippians, Philemon, 1 Timothy, Titus, Hebrews, and 2 Timothy. These Epistles give us a clear view of the carrying out of God's New Testament economy.

Not long after Paul presented a clear view of God's New Testament economy by completing his writings of the divine revelation, he was martyred. Approximately a quarter of a century later, the book of Revelation was written. In the seven epistles of Revelation 2 and 3 we can see that the churches, which had been established mainly by Paul for the accomplishment of God's New Testament economy by propagating the resurrected Christ, had become degraded. The degradation consisted of the loss of the all-inclusive Christ and the taking in of other things as replacements of Christ. With the exception of the epistle to the church in Philadelphia, we see that in these seven churches various things had crept in to replace Christ.

Almost nineteen centuries have passed since the book of Revelation was written. Throughout these centuries a struggle has been taking place between Satan and God. Satan has been trying in different ways to replace Christ. As a result, many of us, including me, were born into an organized

Christianity that had very little of Christ. For example, how much of Christ is there in the celebration of Christmas? In today's Christianity there is a mixture of truth and falsehood. Very few believers know the truth in a deep and thorough way.

After I was saved, I immediately began to love the Bible and study it. Gradually the light has come through the Word concerning God's New Testament economy. Through the Lord's enlightenment we can see that Paul was burdened for the full revelation of God's New Testament economy. The accomplishment of the divine economy involved Christ's incarnation, human living, death, resurrection, and ascension so that He might propagate Himself by imparting Himself into God's chosen people. In this way God's people may become His sons and the members of Christ to be a corporate Body to express Him. This expression is in local churches in this age and will be in the New Jerusalem in eternity.

This is the vision Paul saw, and this is what we need to see today. Paul's vision concerning God's New Testament economy is fully revealed and developed in his last eight Epistles. Therefore, with the help of the Life-study Messages, we need to study these Epistles, especially Ephesians and Hebrews. Studying Paul's Epistles will enrich our experience of the propagating Christ in God's New Testament economy.

LIFE-STUDY OF ACTS

MESSAGE SIXTY-SIX

THE PROPAGATION
IN ASIA MINOR AND EUROPE
THROUGH THE MINISTRY OF PAUL'S COMPANY

(32)

Scripture Reading: Acts 25:1-27

In the foregoing message we considered Paul's situation in relation to that of the Jewish religion, Roman politics, and the church life. Now we shall consider various matters in 25:1-27, where Luke goes further in presenting a picture of Judaism, the Roman government, and the church life.

THE REQUEST OF THE LEADERS
OF THE JEWS REJECTED

According to 24:27, "When two years were completed, Felix was succeeded by Porcius Festus; and wanting to gain favor with the Jews, Felix left Paul bound." Porcius Festus was the successor of Felix as governor of Judea. In 25:1—26:32 we see that Paul was left to Festus, the successor of Felix.

Acts 25:1-3 says, "Festus therefore, having come into the province, after three days went up to Jerusalem from Caesarea. And the chief priests and leading men of the Jews informed him against Paul; and they kept entreating him, asking for a favor against him, so that he might summon him to Jerusalem, setting an ambush to do away with him on the way." Here we see that the leaders of the Jews begged Festus to bring Paul back to Jerusalem from Caesarea. Two years earlier, the Roman commander had used four hundred seventy soldiers to take Paul from Jerusalem to Caesarea. Now these Jewish leaders entreated Festus to bring Paul back so that they could set an ambush in order to kill him.

Verses 4 and 5 continue, "Festus therefore answered that Paul was kept in custody in Caesarea, and that he himself was about to proceed there shortly. Therefore, he says, let able men from among you go down with me, and if there is anything wrong in the man, let them accuse him." The Greek word rendered "wrong" in verse 5 may also be translated "out of place," "amiss."

We have pointed out in foregoing messages that the record of Acts indicates that Roman politics was corrupt. Nevertheless, Roman law was very strong. Although the politicians in the Roman government were corrupt, they still cared for the law. Therefore, when Festus was asked to bring Paul back to Jerusalem, he considered that such an action was not according to Roman law, and he rejected the request of the Jewish leaders.

DEFENDING HIMSELF BEFORE FESTUS

We have pointed out that, in contrast to the Lord Jesus, it was necessary for Paul to make a defense in order to save his life from his persecutors so that he might fulfill the course of his ministry. In 25:6-8 Paul defended himself before Festus. Verses 6 and 7 say, "And having stayed among them not more than eight or ten days, he went down to Caesarea; and on the next day he sat on the judgment seat and ordered Paul to be brought. And when he arrived, the Jews who had come down from Jerusalem stood around him, bringing many and serious charges against him, which they were not able to prove." Here we see that the Jewish leaders fulfilled Festus' request in verse 5.

Actually, in defending himself before Festus Paul did not say very much. He simply denied doing anything against either Jewish law or Roman law: "While Paul said in his defense. Neither against the law of the Jews, nor against the temple, nor against Caesar have I sinned in anything" (v. 8).

WANTING TO APPEAL TO CAESAR

In dealing with Paul, Festus was a fox and proposed that Paul go up to Jerusalem and be judged there before Festus. Regarding this, 25:9 says, "But Festus, wanting to gain favor with the Jews, answered Paul and said, Are you willing to go up to Jerusalem and be judged there before me concerning these things?" This proposal exposed the corruption of yet another Roman politician. Here again we see the crookedness of the Roman politicians.

Paul was wise and saw through the subtlety of Festus' proposal. According to verse 10, Paul said strongly, "I am standing before Caesar's judgment seat, where I ought to be judged. I have done nothing wrong to the Jews, as you also very well know." Paul's word concerning "Caesar's judgment seat" indicated to Festus that he intended to appeal to Caesar.

In verse 11 Paul went on to say, "If therefore I am doing wrong and have committed anything worthy of death, I do not refuse to die; but if there is nothing in the things of which these accuse me, no one can hand me over to them. I appeal to Caesar." The Greek words translated "hand me over" may also be rendered "grant as a favor," both here and in verse 16. The Caesar to whom Paul appealed was Caesar Nero.

For his defense Paul wanted to appeal to Caesar. Without such an appeal, the apostle Paul might have been killed by the Jews through Festus' unjust handling of him, and thus his life might not have been preserved for the finishing of the course of his ministry. Paul's appeal to Caesar would fulfill his desire to see Rome for the furtherance of the Lord's testimony (19:21; 23:11). Without this appeal, he would have been killed by the plot of the Jews (23:12-15; 25:1-3, 9), and he would not have been able to write his last eight Epistles.

Before his appeal to Rome, Paul had written only six Epistles: 1 and 2 Thessalonians, Galatians, Romans, and 1 and 2 Corinthians. It was during his first imprisonment in Rome that he wrote Colossians, Ephesians, Philippians,

and Philemon. It was after his first imprisonment that
he wrote 1 Timothy, Titus, and Hebrews. Then during his
second imprisonment he wrote 2 Timothy. Without these
last eight Epistles, what a lack the divine revelation would
have had and what a loss the church would have suffered!
His appeal did render a great profit and benefit to the
Lord's interest.

Acts 25:12 says, "Then when Festus had conferred with
the council, he answered, To Caesar you have appealed; to
Caesar you shall go." The council here was the council of the
Roman province, composed of the councillors or assessors
chosen by the governor of the province, with whom the governor usually consulted concerning an appeal like Paul's.

Why was Paul so strong in daring to appeal to Caesar?
Paul was strong in this matter because, as a Roman, he
knew Roman law. He knew that when he appealed to Roman
law, Festus did not have any choice except to honor this
appeal. No doubt, the Roman politicians were corrupt, but
the Roman government had strong laws which gave Paul a
basis to appeal to Caesar.

On two previous occasions Paul stood on the fact of his
Roman citizenship. In chapter sixteen Paul said to his cap-
tors, "They have beaten us publicly, uncondemned, men who
are Romans, and have thrown us into prison; and now they
are thrusting us out secretly? No indeed! But let them come
themselves and bring us out. And the deputies reported
these words to the magistrates. And they were afraid when
they heard that they were Romans" (vv. 37-38). Later, when
Paul was about to be examined by scourging, he said to the
centurion standing by, "Is it lawful for you to scourge a man
who is a Roman and uncondemned? And when the centurion
heard this, he went to the commander and reported it,
saying, What are you about to do? For this man is a Roman"
(22:25-26). Paul knew the value of Roman citizenship. He
knew that Roman law protected those who were Roman
citizens. The law did not give anyone the right to mistreat a
Roman citizen. Now in chapter twenty-five Paul, according
to Roman law, appealed to Caesar.

REFERRED TO KING AGRIPPA

In 25:13-27 Paul's case is referred to King Agrippa. Verse 13 says, "Now when some days had passed, Agrippa the king and Bernice arrived at Caesarea and greeted Festus." This Agrippa was Herod Agrippa II, who reigned over the region north and east of Galilee. He was the son of Herod in chapter twelve and was a Jew by religion.

Bernice, who came with Agrippa, was the sister of Drusilla, wife of Felix (24:24). She was also a sister of Agrippa, with whom she lived incestuously. This again shows the corruption of the politicians in the circle of Roman politics.

Agrippa's status was quite complicated. He had either a Jewish father or a Jewish mother. His sister Drusilla is called a Jewess in 24:24. Because Agrippa was a Jew in religion, Festus was careful in talking to him concerning Jewish matters. In 25:19 Festus said to Agrippa regarding Paul and the Jews, "They had certain questions against him concerning their own religion and concerning a certain Jesus who had died, whom Paul affirmed to be alive." Here we see that Festus was cautious in referring to Judaism.

Although Festus referred Paul's case to Agrippa and conferred with him about it, this case actually was not in Agrippa's jurisdiction. Festus ruled Judea from Caesarea as the center, and Agrippa ruled another region. However, they were relatives and knew each other well. Therefore, when Agrippa came to Caesarea to visit Festus, Festus referred Paul's case to him.

As we read 25:13-22 we see that Festus and Agrippa, officials of the Roman government, were "playing" with Paul's case. When Festus told Agrippa that the Jews had questions against Paul "concerning their own religion and concerning a certain Jesus who had died, whom Paul affirmed to be alive" (v. 19), Festus was merely playing with words. His manner of speaking exposes the kind of person he was. After Festus told Agrippa that Paul had appealed to be kept in custody for the decision of the emperor and that Festus had ordered him to be kept in custody until he was sent up to Caesar (v. 21), Agrippa said to Festus, "I also myself was

desiring to hear the man" (v. 22). Then Festus replied that
Agrippa would hear Paul the next day. The more we study
the conversation between Festus and Agrippa, the more we
realize both the Roman politicians were evil.

Acts 25:23 says, "Therefore on the next day, when
Agrippa and Bernice came with great pomp and entered into
the hall of audience together with the commanders and
prominent men of the city, Festus gave order and Paul was
brought." Luke's description of the way Agrippa and Bernice
came into the hall indicates the kind of people they were.
Once again, no title is given to Bernice. We are not told
whether or not she was the queen. Luke simply says that
they entered into the hall with great pomp.

After Paul had been brought in, Festus said, "King
Agrippa, and all men who are present with us, you behold
this man concerning whom all the multitude of Jews peti-
tioned me, both in Jerusalem and here, shouting that he
ought not to live any longer. But I perceived that he had done
nothing worthy of death; and when he himself appealed to
the emperor, I decided to send him, concerning whom I have
nothing definite to write to my lord; wherefore I brought
him before you, and especially before you, King Agrippa, so
that when the examination has taken place, I may have
something to write. For it seems unreasonable to me, in
sending a prisoner, not also to signify the charges against
him" (vv. 24-27). In verse 26 the Greek pronoun rendered
"you" is in plural and refers to the commanders and prominent men who were present (v. 23). As we shall see, Agrippa
then gave permission to Paul to speak for himself, and he
proceeded to defend himself before Agrippa (26:1-29).

A WITNESS OF CHRIST

In chapter twenty-five of Acts we have a picture of the
situation in which Paul was. As the one standing in the
midst of this situation, Paul was different from the Jewish
people in their religion, from the Roman politicians, and also
from the church in Jerusalem. This picture reveals that Paul
was one who lived Christ. Paul was a genuine witness to

Christ. It is no wonder, then, that the Lord Jesus considered him a witness when He said to Paul, "Take courage, for as you have solemnly testified concerning Me in Jerusalem, so you must also testify in Rome" (23:11). According to 26:16, the Lord had appointed Paul a minister and a witness. Actually, in all his defenses Paul did not say very much concerning Christ. Nevertheless, the Lord Jesus recognized that Paul was solemnly testifying concerning Him.

Paul could testify of the Lord because he lived Christ. As one who lived Christ and was a living testimony of Him, Paul was absolutely different from the Jewish religionists, the Roman politicians, and those in the church in Jerusalem.

We need to be deeply impressed with the fact that in these chapters of Acts Paul was a genuine witness of Christ. We have seen that these chapters describe three categories of people: the Jewish religionists, the Roman politicians, and those weak and compromising ones in the church in Jerusalem. Now with Paul we have a fourth category. In this category Paul stands alone as a person who lived Christ. Paul not only preached the propagation of the resurrected Christ; he lived this Christ. Paul lived a life that was the propagation of the resurrected Christ. What a glory! What a victory! What a gain for the Lord and what a shame to the enemy that Paul both preached Christ and lived Christ! In the center of the enemy's activity stood Paul, a person who lived Christ. The resurrected Christ had propagated Himself by coming into Paul and making him a living witness of Christ.

LIFE-STUDY OF ACTS

MESSAGE SIXTY-SEVEN

THE PROPAGATION
IN ASIA MINOR AND EUROPE
THROUGH THE MINISTRY OF PAUL'S COMPANY

(33)

Scripture Reading: Acts 26:1-32; Eph. 2:14-16; 3:8, 17; Phil.
3:4-8; Col. 3:10-11; Heb. 10:14, 18; Acts 21:20, 23-24

In 26:1-29 Paul defends himself before Agrippa. Then in
26:30-32 we have Agrippa's judgment. Before coming to
26:1-32, I would like to say a further word concerning Paul's
burden in the four Epistles of Ephesians, Philippians, Colossians, and Hebrews.

FOUR CRUCIAL EPISTLES
CONCERNING THE DISPENSATIONAL TRANSFER

In chapters twenty-one through twenty-six of Acts Paul
passed through much suffering, testing, and trial. The Epistles of Ephesians, Philippians, Colossians, and Hebrews are
the expression of what was on Paul's heart during the period
of time of Acts 21 through 26.

As we have pointed out, Paul wrote Ephesians, Colossians and Philippians during his first imprisonment in
Rome. It should have been after this imprisonment that he
wrote Hebrews. We should not think that these Epistles
were written by accident. On the contrary, they were written after a long period of consideration and preparation. I
believe that the two years of being held in custody in
Caesarea were a time of preparation for Paul. The more he
saw of the situation concerning Jewish religion, Roman politics, and the church and compared this situation with what
he had received from the Lord, the more he was burdened to

put into writing the revelation he had seen. Paul did not have the opportunity to speak what was on his heart. No doubt, he intended to find a time in a quiet environment where he could write down the revelation concerning God's New Testament economy. He must have been looking for a chance to put into writing everything he had seen of the Lord concerning the divine economy, and then to send these writings to the churches, where they would be preserved.

We thank the Lord that He gave Paul the time and the place to write Ephesians, Philippians, Colossians, and Hebrews and that we have these four Epistles today. In these four books we see a number of crucial points concerning the dispensational transfer that we have been emphasizing in these messages. This dispensational transfer is a great matter.

ABOLISHING THE ORDINANCES

In Ephesians 2:14-16 Paul says, "For He Himself is our peace, who has made both one, and has broken down the middle wall of partition, the enmity, having abolished in His flesh the law of the commandments in ordinances, that He might create the two in Himself into one new man, making peace, and might reconcile both in one Body to God through the cross, slaying the enmity by it." Here we see that on the cross Christ abolished all the ordinances. No doubt, this abolishing of the ordinances includes the ones concerning circumcision, diet, and the Sabbath.

Although Christ had abolished these ordinances, James in Acts 21 still promoted them. To be sure, the ordinances abolished by Christ on the cross include the Nazarite vow. Do you not believe that when Christ abolished the ordinances He included the ordinances related to vows? If we have the proper understanding of Ephesians 2 and Acts 21, we shall see that what James did in Acts 21 was contrary to what Christ accomplished on the cross. Christ abolished the ordinances, but James held to them and promoted them.

We may say that the matter of abolishing ordinances is a negative aspect of the revelation in Ephesians. On the positive side, we have Paul's word concerning the unsearchable riches of Christ: "To me, less than the least of all saints, was this grace given, to preach to the nations the unsearchable riches of Christ as the gospel" (3:8). For the present, however, we would emphasize that in Ephesians Paul clearly says that on the cross Christ has abolished all the Judaic ordinances of the Old Testament.

COUNTING AS REFUSE THE THINGS OF JUDAISM

In Philippians 3 we see that Paul counted as refuse all the things of Judaism. Although Paul was "a Hebrew of Hebrews" and "as to the law, a Pharisee" (v. 5), he could testify, "What things were gains to me, these I have counted loss on account of Christ. But surely I count also all things to be loss on account of the excellency of the knowledge of Christ Jesus my Lord, on account of whom I have suffered the loss of all things and count them refuse that I may gain Christ" (vv. 7-8). Paul realized that in the sight of God and in the New Testament economy all the things of Judaism were refuse. Paul's word in Philippians 3 indicates the kind of vision that was within him. However, although Paul counted the things of Judaism to be refuse, James, to his shame, continued to promote them.

THE NEW MAN

In Colossians 3:10 and 11 Paul speaks of the new man: "And having put on the new man, which is being renewed unto full knowledge according to the image of Him who created him; where there cannot be Greek and Jew, circumcision and uncircumcision, barbarian, Scythian, slave, freeman, but Christ is all and in all." Here we see that in the new man there is room only for Christ. In verse 11 "all" refers to all the members who compose the new man. Christ is all the members of the new man and in all the members. He is everything in the new man. What a tremendous revelation this is! According to Paul's word in Colossians 3:10 and 11, not the slightest ground remains for Judaism.

THE UNIQUE OFFERING

The book of Hebrews reveals that Christ is everything. Christ is both God and man, and He is superior to Moses, Joshua, and Aaron. As our High Priest, Christ has replaced all the Old Testament offerings with Himself as the unique offering. Christ is the only offering God cares for, and all the Old Testament offerings were simply types of this unique offering. Now that Christ has come, all the other offerings should be terminated, and in fact they have been replaced and terminated. Concerning this, Hebrews 10:14 says, "By one offering He has perfected forever those who are sanctified," and verse 18 goes on to say, "Now where forgiveness of these is, there is no longer an offering for sin." Furthermore, the old covenant has been replaced by the new covenant. Therefore, the things of the Old Testament are over.

I would ask you to compare the revelation in Ephesians, Philippians, Colossians, and Hebrews with James' word in Acts 21. In 21:20 James said to Paul, "You observe, brother, how many thousands there are among the Jews who have believed, and all are zealous for the law." Then James went on to ask Paul to pay the expenses of four men who had taken the vow of the Nazarite: "Four men are with us who have a vow on themselves; take these and be purified with them, and pay their expenses that they may shave their heads; and all will know that there is nothing to the things of which they have been instructed concerning you, but that you yourself also walk orderly, keeping the law" (vv. 23-24). What a contrast there is between James' word and Paul's revelation concerning God's New Testament economy! This comparison should enable us to have a clear view of Paul's situation in these chapters of Acts.

THE IMPROPER USE OF EPHESIANS,
PHILIPPIANS, COLOSSIANS, AND HEBREWS

What kind of messages on the book of Ephesians did you hear before you came into the Lord's recovery? A favorite verse of those who emphasize evangelism is Ephesians 2:8. This verse tells us that by grace we are saved through faith.

Many messages are also given from Ephesians 5:22-25 about wives submitting to their husbands and husbands loving their wives. Often during a wedding a pastor will quote these verses from Ephesians 5. But have you ever heard a message telling you that on the cross Christ abolished all the ordinances, in particular, that He abolished the differences between the races? Although the ordinances and all racial differences were abolished by Christ on the cross, who preaches this word today? Actually, even in the twentieth century, racial differences are still promoted in order to maintain a separation of the races. From this we see that the book of Ephesians is misused by many believers. They select certain verses from this book without caring for God's New Testament economy. Many have never seen that Ephesians is a book concerned with God's New Testament economy.

On the negative side, Ephesians 2 reveals that the ordinances have been abolished. On the positive side, in Ephesians 3 we see that Paul preached the unsearchable riches of Christ so that Christ may make His home in our hearts (vv. 8, 17). Have you ever heard a message on this matter before you came into the church life? Many of those who attended Bible schools and seminaries can testify that they were never taught that Christ with His unsearchable riches desires to make His home in our hearts. How pitiful is today's situation with respect to the profound revelation in the book of Ephesians!

We have seen that in Philippians 3 Paul counted all religious things as refuse. However, today not many use these verses in a proper way. Instead, it is common that verses are taken from Philippians in order to teach the believers to imitate the Lord Jesus by having the same mind that He had.

In Colossians 3 Paul says that Christ is everything in the new man. This matter certainly is not emphasized among today's Christians. Actually, it is difficult to say how most believers apply the book of Colossians.

Christians frequently quote Hebrews 13:8: "Jesus Christ is the same yesterday, and today, and forever." Some even

use this verse in the attempt to argue against the truth that
Christ today is the life-giving Spirit. According to the Scriptures, we teach that, as God, Christ became a man, and then,
as man, He, the last Adam, became in resurrection the life-
giving Spirit (1 Cor. 15:45). Some falsely accuse us of teaching that Christ is always changing, and then they quote
Hebrews 13:8, using it in the attempt to prove that Christ
could not have become the life-giving Spirit in resurrection.
The use of Hebrews 13:8 in such a way indicates that today's
situation is miserable.

The four books of Ephesians, Philippians, Colossians, and
Hebrews have not been used properly and positively by most
Christians for the taking up of Paul's burden in these Epistles concerning the carrying out of God's New Testament
economy. Instead of using these books according to the
intention of the author, many select certain verses and then
interpret them in a way to promote a degraded situation.
This is a sign of the poverty in the so-called churches.
Actually, today's situation is worse than that in Jerusalem
in Acts 21.

BURDENED TO CARRY OUT
GOD'S NEW TESTAMENT ECONOMY

We have pointed out that, during the years he was kept in
custody in Caesarea, Paul had time to consider the situation
of the Jewish religionists, the Roman politicians, and the
believers in Jerusalem and to compare it to the revelation
he had received from the Lord. We also need a time to consider today's situation. I would encourage you quietly to
consider not only the world political situation, but also the
situation in Judaism, Catholicism, and Protestantism. Consider where today's Christians stand in relation to God's
New Testament economy. Are there not many who, like
James, have compromised and who are promoting the things
God has forsaken?

You also need to consider yourself, in particular where
you are in relation to the carrying out of God's New Testament economy. What is on your heart? What have you seen

as a heavenly vision regarding the divine economy? How will you carry out the vision you have seen? Let us all spend time before the Lord in order to be filled with the burden of God's New Testament economy. Once we are filled with this burden, we, like Paul, should be ready to carry it out.

We thank the Lord for the Epistles of Ephesians, Philippians, Colossians, and Hebrews. Paul wrote these Epistles so that God's New Testament economy may be carried out. I hope that we all, through the help of the Life-study Messages, will become saturated with these Epistles. I also hope that we all shall have a clear view of today's situation and need.

As we shall see in chapters twenty-seven and twenty-eight of Acts, it took quite a long time for Paul to travel from Caesarea to Rome. By contrast, today it is very convenient for us to spread God's New Testament economy. Let us all bear the burden for the spread of God's New Testament economy and faithfully carry out this burden.

LIFE-STUDY OF ACTS

MESSAGE SIXTY-EIGHT

THE PROPAGATION
IN ASIA MINOR AND EUROPE
THROUGH THE MINISTRY OF PAUL'S COMPANY

(34)

Scripture Reading: Acts 26:1-32

In this message we shall begin to consider Paul's defense before Agrippa and Agrippa's judgment (26:1-32).

PAUL'S APPEAL TO AGRIPPA
AND HIS LIVING AS A PHARISEE

After Agrippa told Paul that he was permitted to speak for himself, Paul stretched out his hand and began to make his defense, saying, "Concerning all the things of which I am accused by the Jews, King Agrippa, I consider myself fortunate that I am about to make my defense before you today; especially since you are an expert in all the customs and questions among the Jews; wherefore I beg you to listen to me patiently" (vv. 2-3). As we have pointed out a number of times, in facing his opponents it was necessary for Paul to make a defense in order to save his life from his persecutors. By making such a defense to save his life, he would be able to fulfill the course of his ministry.

Paul appealed to Agrippa as being an expert in all the customs and questions among the Jews. The Greek words rendered, "Especially since you are an expert," may also be translated, "Since you are especially expert."

In verses 4 and 5 Paul continued, "Now, therefore, my manner of life from my youth, which from the beginning was among my nation in Jerusalem, all the Jews know, having previously known me from the first, if they were willing to testify, that according to the strictest sect of our religion I lived a Pharisee." Here Paul vindicated himself by saying that, even before his conversion, he was a proper person and lived the strict life of a Pharisee. Of course, in the sight of God Paul was not proper. But humanly speaking, he did live a proper life, and there was no ground for anyone to condemn him.

THE IMPORTANCE OF RESURRECTION

In verses 6 through 8 Paul went on to speak of the resurrection: "And now I stand here being judged for the hope of the promise made by God to our fathers, to which our twelve tribes, earnestly serving night and day, hope to attain; concerning which hope I am accused by the Jews, O king. Why is it judged incredible by you if God raises the dead?" In verse 6 the Greek word translated "for" literally means "upon," "on the ground of." In these verses Paul indicates that, in contrast to the Sadducees, he had always believed in the resurrection. The resurrection was taught in the Old Testament, especially in Daniel 12. It is a matter that requires our careful consideration.

In the Bible resurrection implies the coming judgment, and judgment implies eschatology. Resurrection, therefore, is related to one's eternal future, whether he will be happy in eternity or suffer perdition. A person's eternal future depends upon judgment, and judgment requires resurrection. From this we see that resurrection is an important matter in the Scriptures, for it concerns our eternal destiny. Even before his conversion, Paul, as a Pharisee, believed in resurrection.

The Lord Jesus spoke clearly concerning resurrection in John 5:28 and 29: "An hour is coming in which all who are in the tombs shall hear His voice, and shall come forth: those who have done the good to the resurrection of life, and those who have done the evil to the resurrection of judgment." We have seen that the resurrection of life is the resurrection of the saved believers before the millennium (Rev. 20:4, 6; 1 Cor. 15:23, 52; 1 Thes. 4:16). The dead believers will be resurrected to enjoy eternal life at the coming back of the Lord Jesus. The resurrection of judgment is the resurrection of the perished unbelievers after the millennium (Rev. 20:5, 12). All the dead unbelievers will be resurrected after the thousand years to be judged at the great white throne (Rev. 20:11-15). Even before he was saved, Paul believed in the resurrection of life and of judgment, as taught in Daniel 12:2.

DOING MANY THINGS CONTRARY TO THE NAME OF JESUS

In 26:9 through 11 Paul admitted to Agrippa that he did many things contrary to the name of Jesus: "I therefore thought to myself that I ought to do many things contrary to the name of Jesus the Nazarene; which also I did in Jerusalem; and many of the saints I shut up in prisons, having received authority from the chief priests; and when they were being done away with, I cast a vote against them. And in all the synagogues, punishing them often, I compelled them to blaspheme; and being exceedingly enraged against them, I persecuted them even as far as foreign cities." Literally, the Greek word translated "foreign" in verse 11 means "outside." Paul not only opposed Jesus the Nazarene—he attacked Him. In his blindness, Paul considered the Lord Jesus nothing more than a poor Nazarene. He attacked the name of Jesus the Nazarene to such an extent that he put many of the saints in prison. Now before Agrippa he confessed his foolish deeds.

THE LORD'S APPEARING

Paul then went on to tell Agrippa that while he was on the way to persecute those who called on the name of the Lord Jesus, he himself was gained by the Lord. "Engaged in which, I journeyed to Damascus with authority and a commission from the chief priests. And at midday, on the way, I saw, O king, a light from heaven beyond the brightness of the sun, shining around me and those who journeyed with me. And when we all fell to the ground, I heard a voice saying to me in the Hebrew dialect, Saul, Saul, why are you persecuting Me? It is hard for you to kick against the goads. And I said, Who are You, Lord? And the Lord said, I am Jesus whom you are persecuting" (vv. 12-15). We have strongly emphasized the fact that this "Me" is corporate, comprising Jesus the Lord and all His believers. We have also seen that spontaneously Paul called Jesus Lord, even without knowing Him.

APPOINTED A MINISTER AND A WITNESS

When the Lord Jesus appeared to Paul, He commissioned him, appointing him a minister and a witness. Concerning this, the Lord said to him, "Rise up and stand on your feet; for I have appeared to you for this purpose, to appoint you a minister and a witness both of the things in which you have seen Me, and the things in which I will appear to you" (v. 16). Here we see that the Lord appointed Paul both a minister and a witness. A minister is for the ministry; a witness is for the testimony. Ministry is mainly related to the work, to what the minister does. Testimony is related to the person, to what the witness is.

We need to be impressed with the fact that what the ascended Christ wants to use to carry out His heavenly ministry for the propagating of Himself so that the kingdom of God might be established for the building up of the churches for His expression is not a group of preachers trained by man's teaching to do a preaching work. Rather, the Lord wants to use a body of His witnesses, who bear a living testimony of the incarnated, crucified, resurrected, and ascended Christ. According to the book of Acts, Satan could instigate the Jewish religionists and utilize the Gentile politicians to bind the apostles and their evangelical ministry, but he could not bind Christ's living witnesses and their living testimony. The more the Jewish religionists and the Gentile politicians bound the apostles and their evangelical ministry, the stronger and brighter these witnesses of Christ and their living testimony became. In His appearing to Paul on the way to Damascus, the Lord clearly told him that He appointed him not only a minister but also a witness. We have seen that as a living witness of Christ, Paul had testified concerning Him in Jerusalem and would testify of Him in Rome (23:11).

In 1:8 the Lord said to the disciples, "You shall receive power when the Holy Spirit has come upon you, and you shall be My witnesses both in Jerusalem, and in all Judea and Samaria, and unto the remotest part of the earth." Witnesses are those who bear a living testimony of the resurrected and ascended Christ in life. They differ from preachers who merely preach doctrines in letters. As recorded in Acts, the ascended Christ carries out His ministry in the heavens through these witnesses in His resurrection life and with His ascension power and authority to spread Himself as the development of the kingdom of God unto the remotest part of the earth.

In all the trials through which he passed Paul was not merely teaching or ministering; he was continually bearing a testimony. He was a testimony before the opposing Jews and before the commander of the Roman soldiers. Paul was a testimony before Felix, the governor of Judea, and before Festus, who succeeded Felix as governor. Now in Acts 26 we see that Paul is once again a living witness, this time before Agrippa. However, Paul did not preach to Agrippa saying, "King Agrippa, you must know that I am a witness of Christ." Instead of speaking this way, Paul testified to Agrippa that the Lord had met him and appointed him a minister and a witness.

A WITNESS OF THE THINGS IN WHICH WE SEE CHRIST

In verse 16 the Lord Jesus said to Paul, "I have appeared to you for this purpose, to appoint you a minister and a witness both of the things in which you have seen Me, and the things in which I will appear to you." Notice that here the phrase "in which" is used twice. Here Paul is saying that the Lord had appointed him a minister and a witness of the things He revealed to Paul and of the things He would reveal to him. Although this is Paul's meaning, this is not the way he presented the matter. Rather, this verse speaks of the things in which Paul had seen the Lord and of the things in which the Lord would yet appear to him.

Acts 26:16 indicates that Paul did not receive the revelation of things without seeing Christ. Instead, he received the things in which he saw Christ. In other words, Christ did not reveal things to Paul without Himself as the content of those things. This is the reason that Paul would be a witness of the things in which he had seen the Lord. In all the visions Paul saw he saw Christ. Furthermore, he would be a witness of the things in which the Lord was yet to appear to him. Here the Lord seemed to be saying to Paul, "In all the visions and revelations you will receive, I shall appear to you." This indicates that if we only see visions and revelations and do not see the Lord, then what we see is vanity.

We do not agree with studying the Bible merely in a theological way. Those who study the Bible in this way may learn theology, but they do not see Christ. There is a great difference between studying the Bible to learn theology and studying the Bible in order to see Christ.

As Paul was on the way to Damascus, Christ revealed certain things to him, and in those things Paul saw Christ. The Lord indicated that He would reveal more things to Paul, and in those things the Lord Himself would appear to him. Therefore, what Paul saw was not merely the things themselves, but Christ as the One appearing in all these things.

In your experience you may claim to receive light from the Lord or to see a vision or revelation. However, you need to consider if Christ has appeared to you in that light, vision, or revelation. In the supposed light, vision, or revelation, have you seen Christ?

Sometimes brothers have come to me excited about some supposed new light they have received. For example, a brother once said, "I praise the Lord that today during morning watch I saw some new light." When I asked concerning the light he had seen, he replied, "I have been enlightened to see that I should cut my hair short." I asked him what the significance of such light was, and he said that cutting his hair short would make him more clean. To this I replied, "What is wrong with having your hair somewhat longer? The Nazarites in the Old Testament kept their hair long. Then at the conclusion of their vow, they shaved their heads, and in this way they were cleansed. It seems that your way of cutting your hair is not as good as that of the Nazarites." I spoke to the brother in this way concerning the light he claimed to receive from the Lord because the so-called light was without Christ.

In any light we receive of the Lord we must see Christ. Christ must appear to us in whatever we see in the way of enlightenment, vision, or revelation. If we see a vision without seeing Christ, that vision means nothing. Likewise, if we study the Bible and gain knowledge of the Scriptures without seeing Christ, that knowledge is vanity. We all need to learn to see Christ in the things that are revealed to us.

I appreciate the phrase "in which" that is used twice in 26:16. The Lord first spoke of "the things in which you have seen Me." Then He went on to speak of "the things in which I will appear to you." Here the Lord was saying to Paul, "I will not merely reveal certain things to you, but in the things revealed I Myself will appear to you."

The book of Revelation is an excellent illustration of the Lord appearing in the things revealed to the apostle John. John saw a number of visions, but in these visions the Lord Himself appeared to him. Consider the first vision in Revelation, the vision of the golden lampstands. Concerning this vision, John says, "I turned to see the voice that spoke with me; and having turned I saw seven golden lampstands, and in the midst of the lampstands One like the Son of Man..." (Rev. 1:12-13a). In this vision of the lampstands John saw the Lord walking among the lampstands as the High Priest dressing the lamps.

In another vision the Lord showed John God's universal administration. Regarding this, John says, "After these things I saw, and behold, a door opened in heaven, and the first voice which I heard was like a trumpet speaking with me, saying, Come up here, and I will show you what must take place after these things. Immediately I was in spirit; and behold, there was a throne set in heaven, and One sitting upon the throne" (Rev. 4:1-2). John went on to say that in this vision he "saw in the midst of the throne and of the four living creatures, and in the midst of the elders, a Lamb standing as having been slain, having seven horns and seven eyes, which are the seven Spirits of God, sent forth into all the earth" (Rev. 5:6). Once again, in the things that were revealed to John he saw the Lord.

In principle, our experience today should be the same as that of Paul and John. Suppose that in your study of the New Testament you claim to have some understanding of Ephesians 5. However, the crucial question is this: Do you see Christ in Ephesians 5? If you see only the matter of husbands loving their wives and wives submitting to their husbands but do not see Christ, then your understanding of Ephesians 5 is very poor, even vain. You may know certain teachings in the Bible, but in those teachings you do not see Christ. You may learn the doctrines of the Scriptures, but in those things Christ has not appeared to you. May we all learn the importance of seeing Christ in the things that we claim to see and know in the Word.

Our consideration of the phrase "in which" in Acts 26:16 may be helpful in showing us the way to study the Bible. In our reading of the Scriptures, we need to dwell on matters such as this. If we spend time to consider the phrase "in which" used twice in 26:16, we shall realize how marvelous it was for the Lord to say to Paul that He had appointed him a minister and a witness both of the things in which he had seen the Lord and of the things in which the Lord would appear to him.

LIFE-STUDY OF ACTS

MESSAGE SIXTY-NINE

THE PROPAGATION
IN ASIA MINOR AND EUROPE
THROUGH THE MINISTRY OF PAUL'S COMPANY

(35)

Scripture Reading: Acts 26:1-32

In this message we shall continue to consider Paul's defense before Agrippa (26:1-29). Then we shall go on to see Agrippa's judgment concerning Paul's case (26:30-32).

In his defense before Agrippa, Paul testified of the Lord's appearing to him and saying, "Rise up and stand on your feet; for I have appeared to you for this purpose, to appoint you a minister and a witness both of the things in which you have seen Me, and the things in which I will appear to you; taking you out from the people and from the Gentiles, to whom I send you" (vv. 16-17). We have seen that Paul was appointed not only a minister but also a witness. In verse 17 the Lord told Paul that He would take him out from the people and from the Gentiles. This verse may also be translated "delivering you from the people and from the Gentiles."

THE CONTENTS OF PAUL'S COMMISSION

To Open People's Eyes

In verse 18 we have the contents of Paul's commission: "To open their eyes, to turn them from darkness to light and from the authority of Satan to God, that they may receive forgiveness of sins and an inheritance among those who have been sanctified by faith in Me." Here the opening of people's eyes is the carrying out of the fulfillment of God's jubilee, the acceptable year of the Lord, proclaimed by the Lord Jesus in Luke 4:18-21 according to God's New Testament economy. The acceptable year of the Lord in Luke 4:19 is the New Testament age typified by the year of jubilee (Lev. 25:8-17), which is the time when God accepts the returned captives of sin (Isa. 49:8; 2 Cor. 6:2) and when the oppressed under the bondage of sin may enjoy the release of God's salvation. The first item of the spiritual and divine blessings of the New Testament jubilee, which are the blessings of the gospel of God, is to open the eyes of those who are fallen and turn them from darkness to light so that they may see the divine things in the spiritual realm. To see these things requires spiritual sight and divine light.

Many of us have had the experience of listening to certain messages that brought us into darkness and of listening to other messages that brought us into light. Suppose you are listening to a sermon given by a particular minister, pastor, or preacher. The more you listen to that sermon, the more you are brought into darkness, and everything becomes opaque. However, you may listen to another message, and the more you listen, the more the divine light shines in you. Day dawns, your eyes are opened, and you begin to see spiritual things. This is the kind of message that opens people's eyes.

Turning from Darkness to Light and from the Authority of Satan to God

Acts 26:18 speaks not only of the opening of the eyes but also of the turn from darkness to light and from the authority of Satan to God. This turn is what we mean by a transfer. To turn from darkness to light is to have a transfer from darkness into light, and to turn from the authority of Satan to God is to be transferred out of the authority of Satan into God. What a great transfer this is!

Darkness is a sign of sin and death; light is a sign of righteousness and life (John 1:4; 8:12). The authority of Satan is Satan's kingdom (Matt. 12:26), which belongs to darkness. Satan is the ruler of this world (John 12:31) and the ruler of the power of the air (Eph. 2:2). He has his authority and his angels (Matt. 25:41), who are his subordinates as principalities, powers, and rulers of the darkness of this world (Eph. 6:12). Hence, Satan has his kingdom, the authority of darkness (Col. 1:13).

According to 26:18, we are transferred from the authority of Satan to God. Actually, to be transferred to God is to be transferred to the authority of God, which is God's kingdom belonging to light. Formerly we were in darkness and under the authority of Satan. But we have been transferred out of darkness and the authority of Satan into light and God.

Darkness is actually the authority of Satan. Whenever we are in darkness, we are under the satanic authority. Light is God Himself (1 John 1:5). Therefore, when we are in the light, we are in God. Just as Satan and darkness are one, so God and light are one. The greatest transfer we can have is the transfer from darkness to light.

In chapter twenty-one of Acts James was promoting the old things of Judaism. When he was doing this, he was in darkness. James said to Paul, "You observe, brother, how many thousands there are among the Jews who have believed, and all are zealous for the law" (21:20). This word was spoken in darkness, and it indicates that James himself was blind and in darkness. Because he was in darkness, he was also under the authority of Satan. It is not too severe to say this concerning James.

Paul certainly was not blind. However, in Acts 21 he was in danger of being pulled back into darkness. Actually, for the days he was in the temple with the others for the completion of the Nazarite vow, he was in darkness.

The Forgiveness of Sins

In 26:18 we see that when our eyes are opened and we have a turn, a transfer, from darkness and satanic authority to light and God, we may receive forgiveness of sins. Forgiveness of sins is the base of all the blessings of the New Testament jubilee. The genuine forgiveness of sins comes through the opening of the eyes and the transfer from Satan to God. Therefore, we need to have our eyes opened and to have a transfer from the authority of Satan to God in order to receive the complete and perfect forgiveness of sins.

The Divine Inheritance

Christ as the Embodiment of the Triune God

As the result of having our eyes opened and of being transferred from the authority of Satan to God, we not only have the forgiveness of sins on the negative side, but also we receive an inheritance on the positive side. This divine inheritance is the Triune God Himself with all that He has, all He has done, and all He will do for His redeemed people. This Triune God is embodied in the all-inclusive Christ (Col. 2:9), who is the portion allotted to the saints as their inheritance (Col. 1:12). The Holy Spirit, who has been given to the saints, is the foretaste, the seal, the pledge, and the guarantee of this divine inheritance (Rom. 8:23; Eph. 1:13-14), which we are sharing and enjoying today in God's New Testament jubilee as a foretaste, and will share and enjoy in full in the coming age and for eternity (1 Pet. 1:4). In the type of the jubilee in Leviticus 25:8-13, the main blessings were the liberty proclaimed and the returning of every man unto his own inheritance. In the fulfillment of the jubilee here, liberation from the authority of darkness and receiving the divine inheritance are also the primary blessings.

Believers are generally taught that the inheritance in Acts 26:18 is a heavenly mansion. This is what I was told as a young Christian. But after more than fifty years of studying the Bible, I have learned that this inheritance is Christ as the embodiment of the processed Triune God. This Christ is the portion of the saints. In Colossians 1:12 Paul says that the Father has qualified Us "for a share of the portion of the saints in the light." This portion is the "lot," the inheritance, of the saints. The inheritance is a lot, and this lot is a portion.

In the Old Testament the twelve tribes of Israel each received an allotment, a portion, of the good land for an inheritance. The good land is a type of the all-inclusive Christ given to us as our inheritance. Therefore, Christ, the embodiment of the processed Triune God, is our inheritance. This inheritance is the processed Triune God fully embodied in the all-inclusive Person of Christ, who through resurrection has become the life-giving Spirit.

Among Those Who Are Sanctified

According to Acts 26:18, the divine inheritance is among those who have been sanctified by faith in Christ. This sanctification is not only positional but also dispositional (Rom. 6:19, 22). Sanctification (being made holy) is not only a matter of position, that is, not only a matter of being separated from a common, worldly position to a position for God, as illustrated in Matthew 23:17 and 19, where the gold is sanctified by the temple and the gift is sanctified by the altar through a change of position, and in 1 Timothy 4:3-5, where food is sanctified by the saints' prayer. Sanctification is also a matter of disposition, that is, a matter of being transformed from the natural disposition to a spiritual one, as mentioned in 2 Corinthians 3:18 and Romans 12:2. This involves a long process, beginning from regeneration (1 Pet. 1:2-3; Titus 3:5), passing through the whole Christian life (1 Thes. 4:3; Heb. 12:14; Eph. 5:26), and being completed at the time of rapture, at the maturity of life (1 Thes. 5:23).

To be sanctified positionally is only to have a change in position and usage; to be sanctified dispositionally is to be transformed in nature by and with the holy nature of God. Sanctification is a saturation with God as our possession for our enjoyment today. It will consummate in our maturity in the divine life so that we may resemble God and be qualified to fully possess and enjoy Him as our inheritance in the coming age and for eternity.

NOT DISOBEDIENT TO THE HEAVENLY VISION

In 26:19 and 20 Paul testified, "Wherefore, King Agrippa, I was not disobedient to the heavenly vision, but declared first to those in Damascus and also in Jerusalem and all the country of Judea, and to the Gentiles, that they should repent and turn to God, doing works worthy of repentance."

Paul's use of the word "vision" in verse 19 indicates that Paul was obedient not to doctrine, theory, religious creed, or theology, but to the heavenly vision, in which he saw the divine things concerning the Triune God to be dispensed into His chosen, redeemed, and transformed people. All his preachings in Acts and writings in his fourteen Epistles from Romans through Hebrews are a detailed description of this heavenly vision he saw.

ALLIED WITH GOD

In 26:21 and 22 Paul continued, "Because of these things the Jews seized me in the temple and tried to slay me. Therefore, having obtained the help which is from God, I have stood unto this day, testifying both to small and great, saying nothing apart from the things which both the prophets and Moses said were about to take place." The Greek word translated "help" in verse 22 also means "assistance." The root of this Greek word means alliance. This implies that the apostle was allied with God and realized God's assistance in this alliance.

TESTIFYING THAT THE CHRIST SHOULD SUFFER
AND ANNOUNCE LIGHT

In 26:22 Paul did not say, "I have lived unto this day"; rather, he said, "I have stood unto this day." Paul had stood in front of the Roman commander and in front of Felix and Festus. Now Paul was standing before Agrippa. As Paul stood before Agrippa, he was bold, saying that he testified both to small and great. The great ones to whom Paul testified included Felix, Festus, and Agrippa.

Paul told Agrippa that he did not testify anything apart from the things which both the prophets and Moses said were about to take place, "that the Christ should suffer and that He first, from the resurrection of the dead, should announce light both to the people and to the Gentiles" (v. 23). Literally, the Greek words rendered "should suffer" mean "was to be subject to suffering." Furthermore, the Greek words translated, "He first, from the resurrection of the dead, should announce" may be rendered, "by the resurrection of the dead He should be the first to announce," or, "He being the first to rise from the dead should announce."

In 26:23 Paul says that the Christ announced light both to the people and to the Gentiles. The word "light" here indicates the enlightenment of God, who is light (1 John 1:5), shining in Christ, who is the light of the world (John 8:12; 9:5), through the preaching of the gospel of the glory of Christ (2 Cor. 4:4, 6). Here Paul spoke of light instead of life because both the religious people and the Roman politicians were in darkness. Because they were in a dark "cell," Paul said that Christ first, from the resurrection of the dead, announced light both to the people and to the Gentiles.

FESTUS' REACTION AND PAUL'S REPLY

Acts 26:24 goes on to say, "And as he was saying these things in his defense, Festus said with a loud voice, You are insane, Paul! Your great learning is driving you insane!" The Greek word for "insane" in verses 24 and 25 also means mad, crazy, beside one's self. Literally, the Greek word translated "driving" means turning. Festus, who was the host and not the guest like Agrippa, said with a loud voice that Paul's great learning, his scholarship, was driving him insane. As the host, Festus should not have said anything.

In verses 25 and 26 Paul replied, "I am not insane, most excellent Festus, but I am uttering words of truth and soberness. For the king knows about these things, to whom also I speak freely, for I am persuaded that none of these things has been hidden from him; for this has not been done in a corner." In these verses Paul first told Festus that instead of being insane, he was very sobered and also sobering, uttering words of truth and soberness. Then Paul said that Agrippa knew about these things. Agrippa, as a Jew by religion, knew the things of the Old Testament and of the resurrection. Paul seemed to be saying, "Agrippa already knows about these things, for he is one of the Jews."

In verse 27 Paul addressed Agrippa, saying, "King Agrippa, do you believe the prophets? I know that you believe." As a member of the Jewish religion, Agrippa surely believed the prophets.

In verse 28 Agrippa replied to Paul, saying, "By a little talk are you persuading me to become a Christian?" The Greek word translated "talk" may also be rendered "time." Literally, the Greek word for "become" is "make." In answer to Agrippa's question Paul said, "I would to God that both by little and by much, not only you, but also all those who hear me today may become such as even I am, except for these bonds" (v. 29). Paul's word in this verse is very eloquent.

AGRIPPA'S JUDGMENT

Acts 26:30-32 says, "And the king rose up, and the governor and Bernice and those sitting with them, and when they had withdrawn, they spoke to one another, saying, This man is doing nothing worthy of death or of bonds. And Agrippa said to Festus, This man could have been released if he had not appealed to Caesar." Here we see that in Agrippa's opinion Paul could have been released if he had not appealed to Caesar. However, without this appeal, the apostle might have been killed by the Jews through Festus' unjust handling of him (25:9), and thus his life might have not been preserved to that day. If Paul had not appealed to Caesar, he might not have had the opportunity to write the crucial Epistles of Ephesians, Colossians, Philippians, and Hebrews.

In the section of Acts from 21:27 to 26:32, a long narration of the Jews' ultimate persecution of the apostle, the genuine characteristics of all the involved parties were made manifest. First we see the darkness, blindness, hatred, and hypocrisy of the Jewish religion. Second, we see the injustice and corruption of Roman politics. Third, we have the transparency, brightness, faithfulness, and courage of the apostle. Finally, there is the Lord's encouraging care for His witness and His sovereignty over the entire situation for the carrying out of His divine purpose.

LIFE-STUDY OF ACTS

MESSAGE SEVENTY

THE PROPAGATION
IN ASIA MINOR AND EUROPE
THROUGH THE MINISTRY OF PAUL'S COMPANY

(36)

Scripture Reading: Acts 27:1-44

In chapters twenty-seven and twenty-eight of Acts Luke gives us a long narration of Paul's voyage from Caesarea to Rome. We may wonder why Luke includes such a lengthy and detailed record. In certain matters he is very brief, but the record of this voyage is very detailed and vivid. After considering this matter, I believe that the reason for this detailed account is that Luke intends to present a picture that conveys some important points.

SATAN'S ATTACK

The first of the points conveyed in Luke's lengthy narrative of Paul's voyage is Satan's attack on the apostle. Satan was constantly behind the scene attacking Paul. This is the reason that the voyage was difficult, with many hardships, and took such a long time. The weather in particular was very bad. Acts 27:4 says, "And from there we put out to sea and sailed under the shelter of Cyprus because the winds were contrary." Later, after boarding an Alexandrian ship, they "sailed slowly for a considerable number of days and came with difficulty off Cnidus" (v. 7). Then with difficulty they came to a certain place called Fair Havens. Eventually, after putting out to sea again, "there beat down from the island a hurricane wind called a northeaster" (v. 14). Satan was behind these difficulties, attacking the apostle.

THE LORD'S SOVEREIGN CARE

In the picture portrayed in Acts 27 and 28 we also see the Lord's sovereign care. The Lord is over all things, including the wind and the storms. The Lord was sovereign over the centurion named Julius who brought Paul to Rome and over all the soldiers who were with him. In His sovereignty, the Lord caused this centurion to show kindness to Paul. Concerning this, 27:3 says, "And on the next day we landed at Sidon; and Julius, treating Paul kindly, allowed him to go to his friends to receive care." Probably some soldiers accompanied Paul, and it is likely that Paul was still in chains. Nevertheless, the Lord sovereignly took care of Paul.

In His sovereignty the Lord also sent an angel to Paul in the midst of a violent storm, when those on the ship had abandoned all hope of being saved (vv. 20, 23). Paul testified that the angel had said to him, "Do not fear, Paul; you must stand before Caesar; and behold, God has granted you all those who are sailing with you" (v. 24). As we shall see, this word indicates that there on the boat Paul had a little kingdom composed of two hundred seventy-six citizens.

Luke and Aristarchus, a Macedonian of Thessalonica, were with Paul on the ship. Luke functioned in two ways. First, as a medical doctor, he took care of Paul's health. Second, he functioned as a newsman to record the details of the voyage. We thank the Lord for this record. The more we read it, the more we realize how significant it is. In Luke's detailed account of the voyage we see that the Lord overruled Satan's attacks. Everything that happened took place at the right time so that Paul's life was preserved.

PAUL'S LIVING

The picture in these chapters of Acts also shows Paul's life, behavior, and character. We see Paul's ascendancy over the situation. We also see the wisdom and dignity of his human life. No doubt, Paul's life was a life of living Christ and magnifying Him.

If we read this portion carefully, we shall see that here Paul was living the very life that he aspired to live in

Philippians 3. In that chapter Paul says that he pursued Christ in order to be found in Him (vv. 9, 12). When I read Acts 27 and 28, I find Paul in Christ. Throughout a rough and difficult voyage, Paul lived a life of ascendancy and dignity and full of wisdom. Although he was a prisoner, he behaved like a king. Furthermore, he had foresight and wisdom to handle matters.

No doubt, the Lord was with Paul. On the one hand, he was a prisoner, one among two hundred seventy-six passengers. On the other hand, he was the center, the focus, of the situation, whether on the ship or on the island where they wintered after the ship was destroyed. In every circumstance Paul lived a life of ascendancy.

FORETELLING THE DANGER OF THE VOYAGE

Let us now consider some of the details recorded in 27:1-44. Acts 27:1 says, "And when it was decided that we should sail to Italy, they delivered Paul and certain other prisoners to a centurion named Julius of the Augustan cohort." The pronoun "we" indicates that Luke, the writer, was included. The Augustan cohort may have been an imperial cohort named by Caesar Augustus (cf. Luke 2:1). A cohort was one of ten divisions of an ancient Roman legion and was composed of six hundred men.

Verse 2 continues, "And going on board a ship of Adramyttium, which was about to sail to places along the coast of Asia, we put out to sea, and Aristarchus, a Macedonian of Thessalonica, was with us." This is the beginning of the apostle's fourth ministry journey, which ended in 28:31.

In his account Luke says that at Myra "the centurion found an Alexandrian ship sailing for Italy, and he put us aboard it" (v. 6). Verses 9 and 10 say, "And when considerable time had passed and the voyage was now dangerous, and also because the Fast had already passed, Paul advised them, saying, Men, I perceive that the voyage will be with damage and much loss, not only of the cargo and the ship, but also of our lives." The Fast in verse 9 refers to the day of atonement (Lev. 16:29-31; 23:27-29; Num. 29:7).

In verse 10 Paul voiced his feeling about the danger of the voyage. The sailors were experts in sailing the ship, and they knew all about the wind and the sea, but they did not have the insight that Paul had. Although Paul warned them of the damage and loss they would face, "the centurion was persuaded by the navigator and the ship's owner rather than by what was being said by Paul" (v. 11). The navigator and the ship's owner convinced the centurion not to take Paul's word. Therefore, according to their mistaken concept, they continued the voyage. Paul, of course, was neither a sailor nor a navigator. Rather, he was a preacher who at that time was a prisoner. However, he had more insight than the centurion, the soldiers, the sailors, the navigator, and the owner of the ship. Here we have a view of Paul's character.

THE STORM AND PAUL'S PREDICTION OF SAFETY

Acts 27:13-26 describes the storm and Paul's prediction of safety. Verses 13 and 14 say, "And when a south wind blew gently, supposing that they had obtained their purpose, they weighed anchor and sailed along Crete close inshore. But not long afterward there beat down from the island a hurricane wind called a northeaster." Literally, the Greek word translated "the island" means "it" and refers to Crete.

Verses 15 through 17 continue: "And when the ship was caught by it and was not able to face the wind, we gave way to it and were driven along. And running under the shelter of a certain little island called Clauda, we were hardly able to get control of the small boat, which having hoisted up, they used helps, undergirding the ship; and fearing that they might run aground on Syrtis, they lowered the gear and so were driven along." "To get control of the small boat" was to secure on deck the small boat which, in calm weather, was attached by a rope to the vessel's stern (Vincent). The helps mentioned in verse 17 were things such as ropes and chains. To undergird the ship with these helps was to pass the cables around the body of the ship. Syrtis, on which they feared that they might run aground, was a shoal southwest of the island of Crete. For the sailors to lower the gear means either that they lowered the sails or dropped the sea anchor.

According to verses 18 and 19, they began to jettison the cargo and throw the ship's gear, or furniture, overboard. Verse 20 indicates that the storm was so severe that eventually they lost hope: "Now, when neither sun nor stars appeared for many days, and no small storm was assailing us, all hope that we might be saved was now abandoned." As we shall now see, that time was a good opportunity for Paul to say something to those on the ship.

Concerning this, verse 21 says, "And when they had gone a long time without food, Paul then stood in their midst and said, O men, you should have listened to me and not set sail from Crete and incurred this damage and loss." Although Paul was a prisoner in bonds, his behavior displayed much ascendancy with dignity. Luke's narration, as an account of the Lord's move on earth, does not stress doctrine but the testimony of the Lord's witnesses (1:8). Hence, in his narration there are no details of doctrines but of the events that occurred to His witnesses, in order to portray their testimonies in their lives. It is especially so with Paul's voyage in the last two chapters.

Here Paul was a witness of the Lord. Therefore, we should not read Luke's account merely as a story of a storm at sea. Rather, we need to see in this story the description of the life of one of Christ's living witnesses.

In 27:21 Paul was frank. The others on board the ship did not have a word to say. Everyone, including the centurion and the navigator, was subdued.

In verse 22 Paul went on to say, "And now I advise you to cheer up, for there will be no loss of life among you, but only of the ship." They all had lost heart and were waiting for death. Paul, however, told them to cheer up, assuring them there would be no loss of life but only of the ship. Here Paul seems to be saying, "There will be no loss of life among us, but the ship will be lost. Because you did not listen to me, you will lose your ship."

Verses 23 and 24 continue, "For this very night an angel

of the God whose I am and whom I serve stood by me, saying, Do not fear, Paul; you must stand before Caesar; and behold, God has granted you all those who are sailing with you." In verse 23 Paul indicated first that he belonged to God and then that he served Him. The Greek word rendered "serve" means to serve as a priest.

In verse 24 the angel assured Paul that he would stand before Caesar. This was to fulfill the Lord's promise in 23:11 and the apostle's desire in 19:21.

According to verse 24, God granted to Paul all those who were sailing with him. This indicates that God had given them to Paul and that they were all under him. Apart from Paul's presence with them, they all would have lost their lives. Here Paul seems to be saying, "Because of me, your lives will be preserved. The Lord has given all of you to me."

In verses 25 and 26 Paul went on to say, "Wherefore, cheer up, men, for I believe God that it shall be so, even in the way in which it has been spoken to me. But we must run aground on a certain island." We may regard this word both as an insight and as a prophecy. Paul had the wisdom to see into the situation and to realize what would happen. Because he spoke such a definite word about running aground on a certain island, we may consider this word a prophecy.

THE BASE THOUGHT AND FOLLY
OF THE SAILORS AND SOLDIERS AND
THE ASCENDANT WISDOM AND CARE OF PAUL

In 27:27-44 we have a contrast between the base thought and folly of the sailors and the soldiers and the ascendant wisdom and care of Paul. This indicates that those without Christ are base and foolish. The sailors attempted to flee out of the ship, but they were caught by Paul, who was watching over them like a king. "And when the sailors were seeking to flee out of the ship and were lowering the small boat into the sea under pretense of intending to lay out anchors from the bow, Paul said to the centurion and the soldiers, Unless these men remain in the ship, you cannot be saved. Then the soldiers cut away the ropes of the small boat and let it fall off" (vv. 30-32). Paul told the centurion and the soldiers that they could not be saved unless the sailors remained in the ship. It seems that Paul was the one in charge, giving orders to his "army" to do what was necessary.

Verses 33 and 34 continue, "And until day was about to come, Paul was encouraging them all to take some food, saying, Today is the fourteenth day that you have continued watching without food, taking nothing. Wherefore I encourage you to take some food; for this is for your salvation; for not a hair will perish from the head of any one of you." They had been watching over the storm for fourteen days, and they did not have the heart to eat anything. Now Paul encouraged them to take food, for it would be for their salvation. The word "salvation" here means that without eating the men would not be saved from the storm. They needed to eat in order to have the strength to swim and to do what was necessary once they were on land.

Verse 35 says, "And when he had said these things, he took bread and gave thanks to God before all; and he broke it and began to eat." Here Paul conducted himself like a king, or at least like the head of a large family. He gave thanks for the food and went on to eat. The storm was still raging, the boat was shaking, and they were afraid of losing their lives. Nevertheless, Paul told them to cheer up, to be at peace, and to take some food in order to have the strength they needed. Then, in front of them all, he took the lead to eat. All the others were frightened and did not have the heart to eat. For this reason, Paul set up an example and seemed to be saying, "I am cheerful and at peace. I encourage you to follow me, for I am a man living Christ." Because Paul took the lead to be cheerful and to eat, "all became cheerful, and they took food" (v. 36). According to verse 37, there were in all "two hundred and seventy-six souls in the ship." As we have indicated, they all were actually subjects in the kingdom ruled over by Paul.

In 27:30 the sailors wanted to flee, and in verse 42 the soldiers wanted to kill the prisoners: "Now the counsel of the soldiers was that they should kill the prisoners, lest anyone should swim away and escape." However, the Lord in His sovereignty protected Paul. "The centurion, intending to bring Paul safely through, prevented them from their intention and ordered those who were able to swim to throw themselves overboard first and get to the land; and the rest, some on planks, and others on some of the things from the ship. And so it happened that all were brought safely through onto the land" (vv. 43-44). What the centurion did in keeping the soldiers from their intention was once again the sovereignty of the Lord to preserve His servant's life. Because of the Lord's sovereign protection of Paul, all those on the ship were brought safely to land, to an island called Malta (28:1).

LIFE-STUDY OF ACTS

MESSAGE SEVENTY-ONE

THE PROPAGATION
IN ASIA MINOR AND EUROPE
THROUGH THE MINISTRY OF PAUL'S COMPANY

(37)

Scripture Reading: Acts 28:1-31

In this message we shall cover chapter twenty-eight, the last chapter of Acts. In 28:1-10 Paul comes to the island of Malta and there does many miracles. Then in 28:11-31 he arrives in Rome, ending the fourth journey. First he passes through Syracuse, Rhegium, Puteoli, the Market of Appius, and Three Inns (vv. 11-16). He contacts the Jewish leaders (vv. 17-22) and ministers in Rome (vv. 23-31).

TO THE ISLAND OF MALTA, DOING MIRACLES

Acts 28:1 and 2 say, "And having been brought safely through, we recognized then that the island was called Malta. And the natives showed us extraordinary kindness; for, having kindled a fire, they took us all in because of the rain coming on and because of the cold." The Greek word translated "natives" in verses 2 and 4 also means barbarians, referring to those who spoke neither Greek nor Latin but who are not necessarily uncivilized.

Verses 3 through 5 continue, "But when Paul had collected a bundle of sticks and put them on the fire, a viper came out because of the heat and fastened on his hand. And when the natives saw the snake hanging from his hand, they said to one another, Undoubtedly this man is a murderer, whom, though he has been brought safely out of the sea, Justice has not allowed to live. However he shook off the snake into the fire and suffered no harm." Literally, the

Greek word for "snake" in verses 4 and 5 is "beast." But medical writers used this term to denote poisonous snakes. At first, the natives thought that Paul was a murderer because he was bitten by a viper. However, as verse 6 indicates, they eventually changed their minds concerning him: "But they were expecting that he was about to swell up or suddenly fall down dead. But while they were expecting for a long time and beheld nothing unusual happen to him, they changed their minds and said that he was a god." The apostle was not a god in the superstition of the curious natives, but he expressed, in his living and ministry, the true God, who in Jesus Christ has gone through the processes of the incarnation, human living, crucifixion, and resurrection and who was then living in Paul and through him as the all-inclusive Spirit.

In his teaching as recorded in his Epistles Paul emphasized the matter of walking in the Spirit. Throughout the voyage and now on the island of Malta Paul certainly was walking in the Spirit. He surely lived a life that was the incarnated, crucified, resurrected, and ascended Christ. Paul's living was actually the expression of the life-giving Spirit. In every situation of his daily living, Paul was the expression of the very Christ he preached. He preached the incarnated, crucified, resurrected, and ascended Christ as the life-giving Spirit, and on the island of Malta he lived such a Christ as the all-inclusive Spirit. This is indicated by Paul's word, written later, in Philippians 1:20 and 21a: "According to my earnest expectation and hope that in nothing I shall be put to shame, but with all boldness, as always, even now Christ shall be magnified in my body, whether through life or through death; for to me to live is Christ...." Paul cared only to live Christ and to magnify Him. On the island of Malta Paul lived Christ and magnified Him as the life-giving Spirit. As we read Luke's account of Paul's living, we see that his living was the all-inclusive Spirit as the consummation of the incarnated, crucified, resurrected, and God-exalted Christ.

Verses 7 and 8 say, "Now in the vicinity of that place were

the lands of the leading man of the island named Publius, who welcomed us and gave us hospitality three days in a friendly way. And it came about that the father of Publius was lying down sick with fever and dysentery; and Paul went in to him, and having prayed and laid his hands on him, cured him." Dysentery was a common disease, but it was difficult to cure. However, Paul, who had been living like a king ruling over his kingdom, now became a physician to heal the father of Publius.

Verse 9 goes on to say, "And when this happened, the rest also in the island who had sicknesses came to him and were healed." Here we see that Paul became the physician, and even a savior, to the whole island. All the sick who were brought to Paul were healed.

On the sea in the storm, the Lord had already made the apostle not only the owner of his fellow voyagers (27:24), but also their life-guarantee and comforter (27:22-25). Now on the land in peace, the Lord made him further not only a magical attraction in the eyes of the superstitious people (vv. 3-6), but also a healer and joy to the native people (vv. 8-9). All during his long and unfortunate imprisonment-voyage, the Lord kept the apostle in His ascendancy and enabled him to live a life far beyond the realm of anxiety, but fully dignified with the highest standard of human virtues expressing the most excellent divine attributes, a life that resembled the one that He Himself had lived on earth years before. This was Jesus living again on the earth in His divinely enriched humanity! This was the wonderful, excellent, and mysterious God-man, who lived in the Gospels, continuing to live in Acts through one of His many members! This was a living witness of the incarnated, crucified, resurrected, and God-exalted Christ. Paul in his voyage lived and magnified Christ. No wonder the people honored him and his companions with many honors (v. 10), that is, with the best respect and highest regard!

Acts 28:10 says, "And they honored us with many honors; and when we put out to sea, they put on board the things for our needs." This verse indicates that the natives on the

island of Malta treated Paul and his companions as if they
were members of a royal family. Paul was the king, and Luke
was one of the family.

According to verse 10, the natives put on board everything that was needed for the voyage. The Lord sovereignly
provided food for two hundred and seventy-six people. Any
king must provide food for his people. As a king, Paul
received the supplies from the natives. However, he did not
owe them anything for this, because he had healed so many
of the sick among them. In a sense, the people paid Paul by
putting on board the food supply needed for the voyage.

TO ROME, ENDING THE FOURTH JOURNEY

Through Syracuse, Rhegium,
Puteoli, the Market of Appius, and Three Inns

Acts 28:11 says, "And after three months, we put out to
sea in an Alexandrian ship which had wintered in the
island, with the twin sons of Zeus for its figurehead." The
Greek word rendered "twin sons" is *Dioscuri,* the twin sons
of Zeus, Castor and Pollux. This was the figure of the guard-
ian deity of the sailors affixed to the stern.

After staying three days in Syracuse, they arrived at
Rhegium, and then they came to Puteoli, where they found
brothers (vv. 12-14). In verse 14b Luke says, "And thus we
came to Rome." In verses 15 and 16 he continues, "And from
there the brothers, having heard the things concerning us,
came to meet us as far as the Market of Appius and Three
Inns; and when Paul saw them, he thanked God and took
courage. And when we entered into Rome, Paul was permitted to remain by himself with a soldier guarding him." In
Latin "Market of Appius" is *Appii Forum,* a place over forty
miles from Rome. In Latin "Three Inns" is *Tres Tabernae,* a
place over thirty miles from Rome.

The warm welcome of the brothers from Rome and the
loving care of those in Puteoli (vv. 13-14) show the beauti-
ful Body life in the early days among the churches and the
apostles. This life was a part of the heavenly kingdom life on
the Satan-darkened and man-inhabited earth. Apparently

the apostle, as a prisoner in bonds, had entered the area of the dark capital of the Satan-usurped empire. Actually, as the ambassador of Christ with His authority (Eph. 6:20; Matt. 28:18-19), he had come into another part of the participation in His church's Body life in the kingdom of God on earth. While he was suffering the persecution of religion in the empire of Satan, he was enjoying the church life in the kingdom of God, which was a comfort and an encouragement to him.

According to verse 15, when Paul saw the brothers, he thanked God and took courage. This indicates that the apostle was quite human. Although he was encouraged by the Lord directly (23:11) and he was very courageous all the way in his voyage (27:22-25, 33-36), he still took courage at the brothers' warm welcome. It was in Paul's uplifted humanity with its human virtues that Christ with His divine attributes was expressed in his voyage. He magnified Christ all the way in his adverse situation (Phil. 1:20).

Before Paul arrived in Rome, the brothers there heard news concerning him and his companions and came to meet them as far as the Market of Appius and Three Inns. How did they receive the news about Paul? This is very difficult to decide. Perhaps some brothers from Puteoli, where Paul was urged to remain seven days, brought the news to the brothers in Rome, who then came to meet him. The important matter is that here we see a picture of the church life in ancient times, a church life that was very enjoyable. We need to have such an enjoyable church life today and follow the pattern presented in these verses.

In chapter twenty-eight Paul's desire to see Rome was fulfilled. The Judaizers had tried to frustrate him from going to the Gentiles, but the Lord sovereignly brought Paul to Rome. It was a great matter in the ancient times to make a journey from Jerusalem to Rome. But the Lord brought Paul far into the Gentile world, even into the capital of the Roman empire. Paul must have been full of joy when he arrived in Rome. Outwardly he was in bonds, but inwardly he was full of glory and unspeakable joy.

Contacting the Jewish Leaders
and Ministering in Rome

Immediately after arriving in Rome, Paul contacted the Jewish leaders (vv. 17-22). Paul was wise in doing this. Then Paul began to minister to them. Of course, his ministry was accepted by some and rejected by others.

Paul's being in Rome was a strengthening to the church in Rome, in particular because a good number of Jews had been saved. Paul came to Rome not too long after writing his Epistle to the Romans. A few years after writing this Epistle, he, the writer, came to Rome.

Acts 28:23 and 24 say, "Now when they had appointed a day for him, many came to him in his lodging, to whom he expounded and solemnly testified the kingdom of God, persuading them concerning Jesus from both the Law of Moses and the Prophets, from morning until evening. And some were persuaded by the things which were said, but others did not believe." Here Paul testified concerning the kingdom of God. As we have pointed out, the kingdom of God was the main subject of the apostles' preaching. This is not a material kingdom visible to human sight, but a kingdom of the divine life. It is the spreading of Christ as life to His believers to form a realm in which God rules in His life.

Verses 25 through 27 say, "And when they disagreed with one another, they began to leave, Paul having said one word, The Holy Spirit spoke rightly through Isaiah the prophet to your fathers, saying, Go to this people and say, Hearing you will hear and by no means understand, and seeing you will see and by no means perceive; for the heart of this people has grown fat, and they hear heavily with their ears, and they have closed their eyes, lest at any time they should perceive with their eyes, and hear with their ears, and understand with their heart and turn, and I will cure them." God the Father spoke this word to the stubborn children of Israel in Isaiah 6:9-10. God the Son quoted this word to the rejecting Jews in Matthew 13:14-15. And now God the

Spirit through the apostle repeated this word again to the hard-hearted people. This indicates that in all the moves of the divine Trinity the children of Israel were disobedient to the God of grace. Then He turned to the Gentiles for the carrying out of His New Testament economy in the spreading of His kingdom for the building up of the churches through the propagation of the resurrected and ascended Christ (v. 28).

Acts 28:30 says, "And he remained two whole years in his own rented dwelling, and welcomed all those coming in to him." During this time the apostle wrote the Epistles to the Colossians (cf. Col. 4:3, 10, 18), Ephesians (cf. 3:1; 4:1; 6:20), Philippians (cf. Phil. 1:7, 14, 17), and Philemon (cf. Philem. 1, 9). In Philippians 1:25 and 2:24 and Philemon 22 Paul was expecting to be released from his imprisonment. Probably after two years he was released and visited Ephesus and Macedonia (1 Tim. 1:3), from where it is likely that he wrote the first Epistle to Timothy. Then he visited Crete (Titus 1:5), Nicopolis (Titus 3:12), from where he wrote the Epistle to Titus, Troas, and Miletus (2 Tim. 4:13, 20), from where he probably wrote the Epistle to the Hebrews.

Acts 28:31 says that during the two years Paul was in his rented dwelling in Rome, he was "proclaiming the kingdom of God, and teaching the things concerning the Lord Jesus Christ with all boldness, unhindered." The kingdom of God is one of the emphases of this book. Luke's writing both begins (1:3) and ends with the kingdom of God.

Paul's proclaiming the kingdom of God was the propagation of the resurrected Christ. How do we know this? The fact that the proclaiming of the kingdom is the propagation of the resurrected Christ is proved by the words "teaching the things concerning the Lord Jesus Christ" in verse 31. This indicates that the kingdom of God goes together with the things concerning the Lord Jesus Christ. To teach people the things concerning Christ is to spread the kingdom of God. Therefore, the kingdom of God is actually the propagation of the resurrected Christ.

LIFE-STUDY OF ACTS

MESSAGE SEVENTY-TWO

A CONCLUDING WORD

Scripture Reading: Acts 1:8; 27:20-26, 33-37; 28:15-16, 23-31; Phil. 1:19-21a; Eph. 2:14-18; Phil. 3:2-8; Col. 3:10-11; Heb. 1:1-3; 9:12; 10:9-10, 12, 14; 13:13

In this concluding word to the Life-study of Acts, I shall cover two matters. The first concerns Paul's living as portrayed in Acts 27 and 28; the second concerns the revelation in the four Epistles of Ephesians, Philippians, Colossians, and Hebrews.

A PORTRAIT OF PAUL'S LIVING

Chapters twenty-seven and twenty-eight of Acts do not present anything of doctrine. Rather, in these chapters we have a record of a man living Christ to the uttermost. Paul was imprisoned, bound in chains, and surrounded by guards. The sea was very stormy, and the sailing was rough. Furthermore, Paul was away from his homeland and from most of his friends. Although he was in such a difficult situation, he lived like a reigning king.

Paul's living as presented in these two chapters of Acts reminds us of his word written while he was imprisoned in Rome: "I know that for me this shall turn out to salvation through your petition and the bountiful supply of the Spirit of Jesus Christ, according to my earnest expectation and hope that in nothing I shall be put to shame, but with all boldness, as always, even now Christ shall be magnified in my body, whether through life or through death; for to me to live is Christ" (Phil. 1:19-21a). This describes Paul's living during the voyage from Caesarea to Rome. Regardless of the situation, Paul magnified Christ in his body.

As we ponder the picture in Acts 27 and 28, we see that
Paul was an outstanding witness of Christ. He was the kind
of witness the Lord Jesus spoke about in 1:8: "You shall be
My witnesses both in Jerusalem, and in all Judea and
Samaria, and unto the remotest part of the earth."

In 1:6 the Lord's disciples had asked Him if He would
at that time restore the kingdom to Israel. The Lord indicated that it was not for them to know times or seasons,
which the Father had placed in His own authority. Instead,
after they had received power through the coming of the
Holy Spirit upon them, they would be His witnesses. Paul
was such a witness in Acts 27 and 28. In these chapters
Paul was living among Gentiles. There were very few Jews
on the ship, if any. Everything on that voyage was Gentile.
The food, the environment, and the atmosphere were Gentile. Furthermore, there was nothing Jewish on the island of
Malta. Paul was surrounded by Gentiles and the Gentile
way of living. But in that situation Paul lived like a king in a
palace. I very much appreciate the picture of Paul's living in
these chapters.

We all should live Christ in the way Paul did in Acts 27
and 28. If we live Christ only in a situation that is according
to our culture, character, constitution, and disposition, our
living is not genuine. Here in Acts 27 and 28 Paul lived
Christ in a situation that was altogether contrary to his
culture and character. Many things were disappointing and
discouraging, but Paul nevertheless lived a life of the highest standard. As we have pointed out, in Paul the wonderful,
excellent, and mysterious God-man, who lived in the Gospels, continued to live through one of His many members.
This was Jesus living again on earth in His divinely enriched
humanity. Paul's living, therefore, was a repetition of the
living of Jesus.

After Paul arrived in Rome as described in chapter
twenty-eight, he wrote the Epistles of Ephesians, Philippians, Colossians, and Hebrews. Paul was imprisoned in
Rome twice. The first was about A.D. 62-64, due to the Jews'
accusation (28:17-20). During that time he wrote the Epistles

of Ephesians, Philippians, Colossians, and Philemon. After his release from the first imprisonment, it is likely that he visited Ephesus and Macedonia, and then Crete and Miletus, from where he probably wrote the Epistle to the Hebrews. Paul's second imprisonment, about A.D. 65, was due to Caesar Nero's sudden persecution of the believers.

Paul passed through many things in chapters fifteen through twenty-eight of Acts. Without his experience of the events recorded in these chapters, he could not have written Ephesians, Philippians, Colossians, and Hebrews, or he could not have written these Epistles in such a thorough way.

THE ABOLISHING OF THE ORDINANCES

In Ephesians 2:14 and 15 Paul says, "He Himself is our peace, who has made both one, and has broken down the middle wall of partition, the enmity, having abolished in His flesh the law of the commandments in ordinances, that He might create the two in Himself into one new man, making peace." I believe that what Paul saw and experienced in Acts 15 through 28 caused him to write such a strong word. As he was writing this, Paul may have been saying to himself, "All the ordinances of the law have been abolished. Circumcision, the Nazarite vow, and even the vow I had have been abolished."

Paul may have regretted his vow in Acts 18 and also his circumcising Timothy in Acts 16. If I had been with Paul when he wrote the Epistle to the Ephesians, I might have said, "Brother Paul, I would like to learn of you. Since Christ abolished all the ordinances, why at Lystra did you still circumcise Timothy?" It is possible that if Paul had been asked such a question, he might have said, "I did that quite a while ago, and I am sorry about it. Never again will I circumcise anyone."

By the time Paul wrote Ephesians 2, he was much more thorough than he was when he circumcised Timothy in Acts 16. His experiences in chapters fifteen through twenty-eight of Acts caused him to be more thorough regarding circumcision. I do not believe that apart from his experience in these chapters, Paul could have written such a chapter as Ephesians 2.

It is profitable to compare Paul's word about circumcision in Galatians to what he says concerning the abolishing of the ordinances in Ephesians 2. Probably Galatians was written before Acts 16. In Galatians 6:15 Paul said, "For neither is circumcision anything nor uncircumcision, but a new creation." Actually, this word still leaves some amount of ground for the practice of circumcision. But in Ephesians 2 Paul's word is absolute, and not one bit of ground remains for the practice of circumcision.

Paul learned from all that happened in Acts 15 through 28. I believe that while he was in custody for two years in Caesarea, he reviewed all that had taken place. As he made such a review, Paul may have said to himself, "If there is an opportunity, I would like to write another letter and say something more thorough concerning circumcision than I said in Galatians. I shall not say simply that neither circumcision nor uncircumcision avails anything. Instead, I shall say that all the ordinances, especially the ordinances regarding circumcision, have been abolished. If I could rewrite the Epistle to the Galatians, I would tell the believers that circumcision has been abolished on the cross. I would tell them not to practice circumcision, for it is offensive to the Lord, an insult to Him. We should not continue to practice anything that the Lord has abolished on the cross."

In studying the Bible, we may compare Ephesians and Galatians with respect to the ordinances concerning circumcision. If we make this comparison, we shall see that what Paul says in Galatians is not as strong or as thorough as what he says in Ephesians. In Ephesians 2 Paul does not leave any ground for circumcision.

A WARNING REGARDING THE CONCISION

In Philippians 3 Paul uses a very strong negative term for circumcision: concision. In Philippians 3:2 he says, "Beware of the dogs, beware of the evil workers, beware of the concision." The word "concision" here, meaning mutilation, is a term of contempt for circumcision. Since there is no conjunction used in this verse between these three clauses, they must refer to the same class of people. Dogs are unclean (Lev. 11:4-8), the workers are evil, and the concision are those deserving contempt. The "dogs" refer to the Judaizers. In nature they are unclean dogs, in behavior they are evil workers, and in religion they are the concision, people of shame. Paul certainly is very strong in charging the Philippians to beware of the dogs, the evil workers, the concision. Here Paul is saying that the Judaizers, those who promote circumcision, are dogs.

What do you think Paul would have said if, in the light of his word in Philippians 3:2, he were asked about James? Paul might have said, "James surely is not a dog, but he acted somewhat like a dog. James is my dear brother. Because I respected him, I went to see him. But when he spoke to me, I heard something that was like the barking of a dog."

As we read Philippians 3, we see that Paul was strengthened through his experiences in Acts 15 through 28 and especially through his time in Caesarea. Because of this strengthening, he told the believers to beware of dogs, to beware of the concision. In Philippians he would not even speak about circumcision, but instead used the contemptuous term "concision." How strong he was in writing this Epistle!

When Paul was writing Philippians 3, he was stronger than he was in writing both Galatians and Romans. In Romans 2:28 and 29 Paul said, "He is not a Jew who is one outwardly; neither the circumcision which is outward in the flesh: but he is a Jew who is one inwardly; and circumcision is of the heart, in the spirit, not in the letter, whose praise is not from men, but from God." Here Paul's word about circumcision is actually not very strong. Once again, some ground remained for the practice of circumcision. But in Philippians 3:2 there is no ground for circumcision, which now is called concision, a practice promoted by "dogs."

In Philippians 3:8 Paul says, "But surely I count also all things to be loss on account of the excellency of the knowledge of Christ Jesus my Lord, on account of whom I have suffered the loss of all things and count them refuse that I may gain Christ." The word "refuse" denotes dregs, rubbish, filth, what is thrown to the dogs; hence, dog food, dung. First, Paul charges the believers to beware of dogs, and then he indicates that what these dogs, the Judaizers, minister is dog food. Once again, we see Paul's improvement in his writings.

When Paul was in Caesarea reviewing the past, he may have regretted that he was not thorough enough in his previous writings concerning the Judaic things. He may have said to himself, "Why did I write in such a vague manner? Why was I not more clear and thorough concerning the Judaic things? These things are dog food, circumcision is actually concision, and those who promote these things are 'dogs.'" As we have seen, in writing Philippians Paul was much stronger than he was when he wrote Galatians. In Galatians he spoke of "false brothers" (2:4), but in Philippians he told the saints to beware of the dogs. Paul seemed to be saying, "They are not brothers or even men—they are dogs!" How thorough Paul was in his later writing!

THE NEW MAN, WHERE CHRIST IS EVERYTHING

In Colossians 3:10 and 11 Paul says, "And having put on the new man, which is being renewed unto full knowledge according to the image of Him who created him; where there cannot be Greek and Jew, circumcision and uncircumcision, barbarian, Scythian, slave, freeman, but Christ is all and in all." Here we see not only that there is no natural person in the new man but that there is no possibility, no room, for any natural person. In the new man there is room only for Christ. He is all the members of the new man and in all the members. He is everything in the new man. Actually, He is the new man, His Body (1 Cor. 12:13).

In writing these words, Paul may have said to himself, "I should not have spoken with the brothers in Jerusalem about Jews and Gentiles. I did not go to the Gentiles—I went to God's chosen people. All those who have been saved through my ministry are God's people. He chose them before the foundation of the world. There certainly was nothing wrong in going to them. In the new man there is no Jew and no Greek, only Christ." In Colossians 3:10 and 11 Paul is clear, thorough, and absolute. This clearness, thoroughness, and absoluteness may have been the result of Paul's two years in custody in Caesarea.

Whereas Ephesians, Philippians, and Colossians were written during Paul's first imprisonment in Rome, Hebrews was written after he had been released from that imprisonment. In Hebrews Paul advanced even further. Before writing this Epistle, he may have said to himself, "Why did I say so little in Ephesians about Christ's abolishing all the ordinances? I should have gone into much more detail. Also, my word in Philippians and Colossians was too short. I need to write a longer epistle to show that all the things of Judaism are over and that Christ is superior to these things."

CHRIST AS REVEALED IN HEBREWS

In the thirteen chapters of Hebrews Paul depreciated the things of Judaism. He even cut every crucial matter in Judaism into pieces. In Hebrews Paul indicates that the Jews have God, but the believers have the God-man, Jesus Christ. Paul goes on to point out that the angels are servants. Furthermore, he shows that Christ is superior to Moses, Aaron, and Joshua.

In Hebrews Paul also tells us that there is no longer a sin offering. According to God's will, Christ, the all-inclusive One, is the unique offering. Therefore, in the universe there is only one offering that is according to God's will. In Hebrews 10:9 and 10 Paul says, "Then He said, Behold, I come to do Your will. He takes away the first that He may establish the second; by which will we have been sanctified through the offering of the body of Jesus Christ once for all." This indicates that all the Old Testament offerings have been taken away and replaced by Christ as the unique offering. In Hebrews 10:12 and 14 Paul says, "This One, having offered one sacrifice for sins, sat down forever on the right hand of God....For by one offering He has perfected forever those who are sanctified."

In Hebrews 13:8 Paul says, "Jesus Christ is the same yesterday, and today, and forever." Prior to 13:8, Christ changed in that He passed through incarnation and resurrection. Through incarnation, He put on human nature. This means that He changed from being One who had only the divine nature to the One who now has both the divine nature and the human nature. Once He was merely God, but He changed to become the God-man. Furthermore, in His resurrection He, as the last Adam, changed to become a life-giving Spirit (1 Cor. 15:45). Since passing through the process of incarnation, human living, crucifixion, resurrection, and ascension, Christ has not changed and will not change. Therefore, Paul had the boldness to say that Christ is the same today, yesterday, and for eternity.

In Hebrews 13:13 Paul continues, "Let us therefore go forth unto Him outside the camp, bearing His reproach." Here "the camp" signifies human organization, especially that of Judaism. Paul's word here is based on the fact that Christ was crucified outside the city, outside the camp. Since Christ was rejected and suffered outside the camp, we should go forth unto Him outside the camp. When Paul wrote this portion of Hebrews, he may have been saying to himself, "I was wrong to go back to Jerusalem. Jerusalem was the camp. There was no need to go back to Jerusalem in order to take care of Judaism, for that was to go back to the camp. We should forget Jerusalem and go out of the camp and bear Christ's reproach."

Paul went outside the camp and bore the Lord's reproach. When he was making the voyage from Caesarea to Rome, he was outside of Judaism bearing reproach as one in bonds. But as he bore reproach outside the camp, he magnified Christ.

I hope that we all shall spend time to dwell on the two matters covered in this message—Paul's living as a wonderful witness to Christ and the thoroughness of the divine revelation in the books of Ephesians, Philippians, Colossians, and Hebrews. In these books no ground is left for any kind of mixture. In these Epistles there is room only for Christ.

ABOUT THE AUTHOR

Witness Lee was born in 1905 in northern China and raised in a Christian family. At age 19 he was fully captured for Christ and immediately consecrated himself to preach the gospel for the rest of his life. Early in his service, he met Watchman Nee, a renowned preacher, teacher, and writer. Witness Lee labored together with Watchman Nee under his direction. In 1934 Watchman Nee entrusted Witness Lee with the responsibility for his publication operation, called the Shanghai Gospel Bookroom.

Prior to the Communist takeover in 1949, Witness Lee was sent by Watchman Nee and his other co-workers to Taiwan to ensure that the things delivered to them by the Lord would not be lost. Watchman Nee instructed Witness Lee to continue the former's publishing operation abroad as the Taiwan Gospel Bookroom, which has been publicly recognized as the publisher of Watchman Nee's works outside China. Witness Lee's work in Taiwan manifested the Lord's abundant blessing. From a mere 350 believers, newly fled from the mainland, the churches in Taiwan grew to 20,000 in five years.

In 1962 Witness Lee felt led of the Lord to come to the United States, settling in California. During his 35 years of service in the U.S., he ministered in weekly meetings and weekend conferences, delivering several thousand spoken messages. Much of his speaking has since been published as over 400 titles. Many of these have been translated into over fourteen languages. He gave his last public conference in February 1997 at the age of 91.

He leaves behind a prolific presentation of the truth in the Bible. His major work, *Life-study of the Bible,* comprises over 25,000 pages of commentary on every book of the Bible from the perspective of the believers' enjoyment and experience of God's divine life in Christ through the Holy Spirit. Witness Lee was the chief editor of a new translation of the New Testament into Chinese called the Recovery Version and directed the translation of the same into English. The Recovery Version also appears in a number of other languages. He provided an extensive body of footnotes, outlines, and spiritual cross references. A radio broadcast of his messages can be heard on Christian radio stations in the United States. In 1965 Witness Lee founded Living Stream Ministry, a non-profit corporation, located in Anaheim, California, which officially presents his and Watchman Nee's ministry.

Witness Lee's ministry emphasizes the experience of Christ as life and the practical oneness of the believers as the Body of Christ. Stressing the importance of attending to both these matters, he led the churches under his care to grow in Christian life and function. He was unbending in his conviction that God's goal is not narrow sectarianism but the Body of Christ. In time, believers began to meet simply as the church in their localities in response to this conviction. In recent years a number of new churches have been raised up in Russia and in many eastern European countries.

OTHER BOOKS PUBLISHED BY
Living Stream Ministry

Titles by Witness Lee:

Abraham—Called by God	978-0-7363-0359-0
The Experience of Life	978-0-87083-417-2
The Knowledge of Life	978-0-87083-419-6
The Tree of Life	978-0-87083-300-7
The Economy of God	978-0-87083-415-8
The Divine Economy	978-0-87083-268-0
God's New Testament Economy	978-0-87083-199-7
The World Situation and God's Move	978-0-87083-092-1
Christ vs. Religion	978-0-87083-010-5
The All-inclusive Christ	978-0-87083-020-4
Gospel Outlines	978-0-87083-039-6
Character	978-0-87083-322-9
The Secret of Experiencing Christ	978-0-87083-227-7
The Life and Way for the Practice of the Church Life	978-0-87083-785-2
The Basic Revelation in the Holy Scriptures	978-0-87083-105-8
The Crucial Revelation of Life in the Scriptures	978-0-87083-372-4
The Spirit with Our Spirit	978-0-87083-798-2
Christ as the Reality	978-0-87083-047-1
The Central Line of the Divine Revelation	978-0-87083-960-3
The Full Knowledge of the Word of God	978-0-87083-289-5
Watchman Nee—A Seer of the Divine Revelation ...	978-0-87083-625-1

Titles by Watchman Nee:

How to Study the Bible	978-0-7363-0407-8
God's Overcomers	978-0-7363-0433-7
The New Covenant	978-0-7363-0088-9
The Spiritual Man • 3 volumes	978-0-7363-0269-2
Authority and Submission	978-0-7363-0185-5
The Overcoming Life	978-1-57593-817-2
The Glorious Church	978-0-87083-745-6
The Prayer Ministry of the Church	978-0-87083-860-6
The Breaking of the Outer Man and the Release ...	978-1-57593-955-1
The Mystery of Christ	978-1-57593-954-4
The God of Abraham, Isaac, and Jacob	978-0-87083-932-0
The Song of Songs	978-0-87083-872-9
The Gospel of God • 2 volumes	978-1-57593-953-7
The Normal Christian Church Life	978-0-87083-027-3
The Character of the Lord's Worker	978-1-57593-322-1
The Normal Christian Faith	978-0-87083-748-7
Watchman Nee's Testimony	978-0-87083-051-8

Available at
Christian bookstores, or contact Living Stream Ministry
2431 W. La Palma Ave. • Anaheim, CA 92801
1-800-549-5164 • www.livingstream.com

10-070-001
ISBN 978-0-87083-187-4